Shining Lights

Workbook 6

C1

Melissa Thomson and Carole Allsop

Shaftesbury Road, Cambridge CB2 8EA, United Kingdom

One Liberty Plaza, 20th Floor, New York, NY 10006, USA

477 Williamstown Road, Port Melbourne, VIC 3207, Australia

314–321, 3rd Floor, Plot 3, Splendor Forum, Jasola District Centre, New Delhi – 110025, India

103 Penang Road, #05–06/07, Visioncrest Commercial, Singapore 238467

Cambridge University Press & Assessment is a department of the University of Cambridge.

We share the University's mission to contribute to society through the pursuit of education, learning and research at the highest international levels of excellence.

www.cambridge.org
Information on this title: www.cambridge.org/9781009228305

© Cambridge University Press & Assessment 2025

This publication is in copyright. Subject to statutory exception and to the provisions of relevant collective licensing agreements, no reproduction of any part may take place without the written permission of Cambridge University Press & Assessment.

First published 2025
20 19 18 17 16 15 14 13 12 11 10 9 8 7 6 5 4 3 2 1

Printed in Italy by L.E.G.O. S.p.A.

A catalogue record for this publication is available from the British Library

ISBN   978-1-009-22830-5   Workbook with Digital Pack

Additional resources for this publication at www.cambridge.org/shininglights

Cambridge University Press & Assessment has no responsibility for the persistence or accuracy of URLs for external or third-party internet websites referred to in this publication and does not guarantee that any content on such websites is, or will remain, accurate or appropriate.

CONTENTS

UNIT 1: Part of the art — page 4

UNIT 2: Tell me a story — page 12

UNIT 3: Other side of the coin — page 20

REVIEW 1: Units 1, 2 & 3 — page 28

UNIT 4: You live, you learn — page 32

UNIT 5: Being me — page 40

UNIT 6: Let's celebrate! — page 48

REVIEW 2: Units 4, 5 & 6 — page 56

UNIT 7: Futurology — page 60

UNIT 8: Wild planet — page 68

UNIT 9: Travel bug — page 76

REVIEW 3: Units 7, 8 & 9 — page 84

EXPLORING EMPLOYABILITY — page 88

VOCABULARY BUILDER AND EXTENSION — page 96

TOWARDS PROFICIENCY — page 105

IRREGULAR VERBS — page 111

UNIT 1 PART OF THE ART

VOCABULARY

LEISURE COLLOCATIONS

1 Complete the conversation with the collocations in the box.

> art enthusiast   family gathering
> flying visit   keen participant
> hilarious comedies   perfect venue
> quality time   social whirl   total flop
> unforgettable experience

A: Thanks for coming out. I know I'm only here on a ¹ _____ but it was good to spend some ² _____ together.

B: Aw, thanks. Yeah, life has been a ³ _____ of new people recently, so it was nice to see you. I know we're cousins, but when we meet up at a ⁴ _____, there are so many relatives asking questions, we don't catch up properly!

A: I know! Last time, Uncle Stuart found out I was a bit of an ⁵ _____ and spent the whole meal showing me photos of his painting class. He's a very ⁶ _____ in that class. He showed me over thirty pieces of work and I didn't get to talk to anyone else that evening!

B: I saw! So, let's talk about what we just saw tonight. I loved the festival, the museum was the ⁷ _____, don't you think? It was an ⁸ _____ when they turned out all the lights at the start.

A: It was! Being in the dark really made the films scarier! A horror-film festival in a park or on a beach might be a ⁹ _____!

B: Either that, or some films would seem like ¹⁰ _____! You really need the darkness to get the right atmosphere.

READING AND USE OF ENGLISH

EXAM TASK READING AND USE OF ENGLISH PART 1

1 For questions 1–8, read the text below and decide which answer (A, B, C or D) best fits each gap. There is an example at the beginning (0).

ART in a gallery or ONLINE?

One of my most unforgettable ⁰ _experiences_ was visiting Madrid's famous art gallery, the Prado. Nothing had prepared me for just how ¹ ____ it was to be face-to-face with the masterpieces on display. I was completely overwhelmed.

The primary ² ____ of any gallery is to actively involve the public in the enjoyment and understanding of art. Yet a different way of viewing art has come into being, with museums and galleries putting parts of their collections online. This has ³ ____ cultural treasures available to millions of people who would otherwise be ⁴ ____ the privilege.

I would argue, however, that to truly appreciate any work of art, you have to ⁵ ____ it first-hand. The difference ⁶ ____ partly from texture and size, qualities that are ⁷ ____ from an image on a screen. To ⁸ ____ to a physical work of art, you need to be close to it in a way that allows for an emotional response that is almost impossible in the online space.

0	A	circumstances	B	encounters
	C	contacts	(D)	experiences
1	A	moving	B	sentimental
	C	persuasive	D	convincing
2	A	target	B	idea
	C	occasion	D	purpose
3	A	brought	B	got
	C	made	D	put
4	A	rejected	B	deprived
	C	restricted	D	denied
5	A	regard	B	attend
	C	determine	D	witness
6	A	issues	B	occurs
	C	arises	D	depends
7	A	elsewhere	B	absent
	C	removed	D	invisible
8	A	relate	B	engage
	C	link	D	associate

READING

✓ EXAM TASK — READING AND USE OF ENGLISH PART 8

1 You are going to read an article in which four artists talk about their work. For questions 1–10, choose from the sections (A–D). The sections may be chosen more than once.

Which artist

recommends trying to think like a child when starting on a piece of work?	1
talks about experiencing differing levels of creative energy?	2
says that being eager to investigate is crucial for their work?	3
acknowledges the benefit of not trying too hard to come up with ideas?	4
mentions a false idea about creating art that is commonly held?	5
admits to finding some aspects of their work unexciting?	6
expresses a desire to be as original as possible?	7
says that their best work is not always what is most appreciated by others?	8
explains why they are unconcerned about criticism of their work?	9
confesses to feelings of disappointment when exhibiting their art?	10

What's it like being a *professional artist?*

Four artists talk about their work

A — Lee Baxter

I recognised my gift for art as a young child, messing about with the tools at hand: pencils, crayons, poster paint, etc. Life without the ability to paint seems unimaginable, and inspiration can come from anywhere — from an image that appears in a dream to the endless variety of the clouds above. Then I'll be in a rush to grab my paints to depict what's inspired me. There are also spells of far less intense inactivity, which many artists go through, just waiting to spark up again. I'm a simple person when it comes to what I do, totally at ease sharing it with others. That's what exhibitions are for, as well as an opportunity to show it to buyers – I need an income! But it's also about letting people have their own reactions to each work. Maybe it gets the seal of approval, maybe they pick it apart. I don't take things personally because art's terribly subjective. And if I fretted about things like whether the subjects of my paintings are hackneyed or groundbreaking, it'd hold me back.

B — Toni Saccheri

As an experimental artist, I create sound installations. It's a less conventional form of art, which I explore with the curiosity of a scientist. For me it's vital to do that. I want to question traditional music structures. I'm fascinated by the qualities of noise, of silence, of almost everything we hear. To create something absolutely unique, it's necessary to undo adult preconceptions. You need an urge to go back to the mindset you had before all those assumptions set in. Creating something completely novel is central to my work. Putting my creations on public display for the first time was an unsettling experience though. I had the perfect venue, a spacious contemporary art space typically frequented by art enthusiasts from all over, but the whole thing was a total flop. Very few people showed up, and those that did just didn't seem to get what my work's all about. It took a while to come back from that, and I've gradually developed a thicker skin for similar occasions.

C — Charlie Rockwell

I discovered technology for creating art digitally when I was about ten, and I've been doing it ever since. By my senior year of high school, it was obvious that I loved digital drawing too much not to pursue it as a career. In fact, it's turned out to be fairly lucrative, perhaps because I've got a good grasp of how to exploit social media to publicise my work, and I exhibit on a variety of platforms. To be honest, spending hours on the promotional side of things can get a bit tedious, but it really pays off. There's plenty of scope for imagination in what I do, as it's not just geometric shapes and fantasy worlds that I draw. I do think originality can be a bit overrated sometimes, and creating a vision of something pleasing to the eye that you might want to decorate your home with is more what I'm into. My greatest inspiration seems to come when I'm doing menial tasks like mopping the floor. Maybe, it's a process of letting go and not forcing it.

D — Ash Osman

Whether it's a photo, a painting, a sculpture, or any other type of art, it must have something to say, or by definition, it's meaningless. Painting is my chosen medium, and I've never got so caught up in the mechanics of it that I've ended up creating something pointless. As I drift off to sleep, I imagine myself in front of my latest project, closing my eyes and visualising what I'm working on. I tend to employ this technique particularly when there's a problem I've got to work out, like how to convey my message more effectively, and the next day I've often found a solution. Most people think art's merely a matter of slapping paint on canvas, when, in fact, creating it consumes your whole mind, and all your energy. When you put your work out there, and you have to to make a living, you confront the reality that not everybody understands your art. What I might view as my greatest achievements aren't necessarily the ones the public go for.

GRAMMAR

PRESENT SIMPLE AND PRESENT CONTINUOUS

1 Choose the correct options to complete the text.

My friends ¹ *always record / are always recording* videos of us out together and ² *I admit / I'm admitting* that it really annoys me. ³ *I wish / I'm wishing* they'd just put down their phones and enjoy themselves. We've got tickets to a gig tonight and ⁴ *I guarantee / I'm guaranteeing* you that when the singer ⁵ *comes / is coming* on stage they'll all get their phones out. It's crazy to pay for tickets because ⁶ *they never actually listen / they're never actually listening* to the music, and as soon as the concert ⁷ *finishes / is finishing*, the videos are instantly forgotten about, or even deleted.

2 Complete the table with the words/phrases in the box. Then circle the correct verb tense.

> as soon as   before   constantly   forever
> guarantee   hope   once   predict

Function	Words/phrases used when expressing this function	Verb tense used when expressing this function
Indicating disapproval	_____ _____	present simple / present continuous
'Performative' verbs	_____ _____	present simple / present continuous
Time clauses with conjunctions	_____ _____	present simple / present continuous

3 Complete the post using words and phrases from Exercise 2.

How many of us take hundreds of photos but don't think about why we do this, either ¹ _____ or after we've taken them? Or how many of us don't have any photos of our most cherished moment? A new trending app aims to tackle these two issues. Foto24 asks users to share a photo a day, and we ² _____ that it's going to be the app of the year. This could be for two reasons, that either we're ³ _____ rushing and don't stop to capture the day to day, or that ⁴ _____ you start experiencing every concert and party through a lens, you can't stop. Undertaking Foto24's simple challenge ⁵ _____ that individuals slow down and document their daily lives. We ⁶ _____ you'll give it a go. Let us know how you get on!

4 Complete the sentences with your own ideas. Use the present simple or present continuous.

1. My friend is so annoying when we go to the cinema! She's continually …
2. I'm going to watch a film as soon as …
3. I don't like that in museums people are always …
4. I hope my favourite singer …
5. Sometimes I choose a film before …
6. Once you know something about an artist, their work …

PRESENT PERFECT

5 Match the uses of the present perfect and present perfect continuous 1–5 to the sentences a–e.

1. Present perfect continuous for activities which started in the past and are still happening.
2. Present perfect continuous for activities which have just finished.
3. Present perfect simple with activities that have/ haven't happened.
4. Present perfect simple with activities that have happened a certain number of times.
5. Present perfect simple after expressions like *It's the first time*, *This will be the second time*, etc.

a. This will be the second time I've seen this artist's work.
b. He's been taking a photo every day as a challenge.
c. I haven't been to that photo exhibition.
d. I've seen this band three times.
e. Hi, I've been waiting for you. Come in!

6 Put the words in order to make sentences.

1 checking / I've / for / day. / been / tickets / every
2 He's / loads / times. / in / the / United States / of / played
3 first / will / concert / This / she's / be / ever / here. / done
4 following / Have / her / you / social media / posts? / been
5 city. / The / shows / have / in / been / every / different
6 I've / for / buy button / had / an / my finger / hour! / on / the

7 Choose the correct options to complete the text.

Video mapping ¹ *has become / has been becoming* the coolest event in the 'festival of light' that more and more cities around the world hold each year. To celebrate special events, artists ² *have projected / have been projecting* images at night onto famous buildings such as Edinburgh Castle, Oaxaca Cathedral and the Berlin TV tower, turning them into dynamic canvases. Locals report that video mapping ³ *has made / has been making* them see their city in a new light, and usually for free. Over the past few years, more and more people ⁴ *have also employed / have also been employing* artists to do video mapping in various events, from advertising to the Olympics. This ⁵ *has pushed / has been pushing* the boundaries of creativity, blending technology and architecture, and appears to be an artform that is here to stay. ⁶ *Have you experienced / Have you been experiencing* it yet?

8 >>> STRETCH! Complete the second sentence so that is has a similar meaning to the first sentence, using the word given. Do not change the given word. Use between three and four words.

1 He is an actor. He started at the age of five. **ACTING**
   He _____ he was five.

2 She won't stop tagging me in photos. I hate that! **ALWAYS**
   I hate that _____ me in photos!

3 He is still working on his next album. **NOT**
   He _____ on his next album yet.

4 Video editing is easy when you learn. **HOW**
   Once _____ edit videos, it's easy.

5 When tickets go on sale, we should get them. **SOON**
   Let's get tickets _____ go on sale.

VOCABULARY
ARTS ADJECTIVES

1 Complete the table with the adjectives in the box.

disjointed   far-fetched   gripping
groundbreaking   hackneyed   harrowing
moving   overrated   tedious   unconvincing

Positive description	Negative description

2 Complete the article with words from Exercise 1.

CAN WE RECOGNISE 'REAL' ART?

It isn't ¹ _____ to say that everyone knows someone who looks at modern art and says, 'It's ² _____. My kid could have done that.' However, research shows even the under-sevens can distinguish works by artists from those of children and animals. In a ³ _____ study, cognitive scientists showed participants unlabelled paired images, one by an abstract expressionist and the other by a child or monkey and asked which was more ⁴ _____ and therefore the one they deemed better. Curiously, when the art was labelled, children made comments such as 'it's good for a monkey', yet selected artist images when making quality judgments, showing that drawings by children are ⁵ _____ in comparison to real abstract art. From now on, art enthusiasts can respond to the ⁶ _____ phrase that even children can match the greats by simply saying, 'No, they couldn't have done that'.

LISTENING

1 Think about the books you read as a child. Describe the illustrations that you liked.

EXAM TIP

Focus more on the question and not the possible answers as you listen. Try to answer the question based on what you hear.

EXAM TASK — LISTENING PART 3

2 🔊 1.1 You will hear an interview in which two artists who illustrate children's books, Leo McAvoy and Polly Wang, are talking about their work. For questions 1–6, choose the answer (A, B, C or D) which fits best according to what you hear.

1 What does Leo say about deciding to become a professional illustrator for children's books?
   A He was influenced by the comments of people whose opinions he trusted.
   B He had a sudden realisation that it was the right option for him.
   C He was unsure about having such an unconventional career.
   D He had a desire to combine his different interests.

2 What is important for Polly in developing her style when illustrating a book?
   A knowing that her best work has a humorous focus
   B receiving plenty of guidance about how to perfect it
   C experimenting with a wide variety of techniques
   D analysing exactly what is required for that piece of work

3 How does Polly feel about the book she's working on at the moment?
   A anxious to maintain the same level of quality throughout
   B enthusiastic about doing the research that is necessary
   C relieved that it is less demanding than it seemed initially
   D determined to prove that she was the right choice of artist

4 What does Leo find the biggest challenge when beginning a new project?
   A meeting the demands of the other people involved
   B working out what themes to use in his designs
   C ensuring that it reflects modern trends
   D interpreting the aims of the written story

5 What do Polly and Leo agree can be helpful for getting over creative blocks?
   A looking at the work of other artists
   B stepping away from their work for a while
   C spending some time with young children
   D setting themselves small targets

6 When asked about illustrating for older children, what do Polly and Leo both say?
   A They find it easier due to the need for fewer items.
   B They have to deal with more challenging topics.
   C They take longer to get a feel for the story.
   D They use more sophisticated approaches.

3 **Emotional Intelligence** What do Polly and Leo find challenging about their job? Think of practical ways to support them with these challenges.

WRITING

A REVIEW

1 Read the task. What kind of review does it ask you to write?

EXAM TASK — WRITING PART 2

An arts website has asked you to write a review of an exhibition you visited, describing what was on display, and explaining which aspects of the exhibition were the most interesting. You should also suggest at least one way in which you feel the exhibition could have been improved.

Write your review. Write your answer in 220–260 words.

EXAM TIP

Including a variety of adverbs of attitude in your review can help show your opinion.

2 Complete the model answer with the words and phrases from the box.

> barely   beautifully conveyed   generally well-managed
> hopefully   hugely interactive   impressively varied
> particularly fascinating   truly amazed

I recently visited the *Wide World* exhibition at the Thomas Art Gallery. I was ¹_____ at the display of contemporary art by international artists, from South and Central America, Australia, Africa, and Europe. The exhibition featured a diverse range of artworks that included paintings, sculptures, and digital installations.

One ²_____ aspect of the exhibition was its thematic unity, despite the diversity of styles. One of the works that stood out most was Jules Blanc's large-scale watercolour painting that ³_____ different aspects of light on nature. Another highlight was the ⁴_____ digital installation by Katya Wlodek, where visitors could adjust colours and patterns on a screen, allowing for more active participation in art.

While the exhibition was ⁵_____, one area where it could have been improved would have been by providing more information about the artists and their works. Although the names of the artists, where they were from and the date and name of the work with the materials used were all given, there was ⁶_____ anything else to help viewers understand the work or the artist's intentions. A brief guide for each work giving some context and detail would have deepened my understanding of each piece and enhanced the exhibition overall. I'm sure many others who visited the exhibition would agree.

In conclusion, *Wide World* was a visually stimulating and thought-provoking exhibition notable for the ⁷_____ work on display. By offering more information, future exhibitions could ⁸_____ further improve the audience's appreciation of the artworks that are exhibited.

3 Read the task again and plan your review. Make notes for each paragraph.

1	Introduction (e.g. where, when, what was on display)	
2	Explain the most interesting aspects	
3	Suggest how it could be improved	
4	Sum up and make a recommendation	

4 Now write your review. Use 220–260 words.

SELF-EVALUATION

Check your writing:

Content: Have you covered all the points asked for? Have you written about interesting aspects and improvements? ☹ 😐 😑 ☺

Communication: Can the reader clearly see your opinion of the exhibition? Is the style appropriate for a review? ☹ 😐 😑 ☺

Organisation: Is the text well-organised and linked? Is there a good flow of ideas? ☹ 😐 😑 ☺

Language: Have you used a variety of structures and vocabulary? Have you included some new language form this unit? ☹ 😐 😑 ☺

GIVING A PRESENTATION

1 PLANNING

I'm going to do a three-minute presentation. Three pieces of art/music/literature I could present are ...

_____
_____
_____

After sharing ideas with a group I've decided to present ...

_____
_____

To present this I'll need to bring ...

_____
_____

TIP If you sound interested, your audience will be interested!

USING YOUR VOICE EFFECTIVELY

How can you use your voice effectively? What do you remember from Unit 1?

- _____
- _____
- _____
- _____
- _____
- _____

Think of the last two presentations you have done. Did you use your voice well? What could be better?

_____
_____
_____

2 USING YOUR VOICE EFFECTIVELY

What phrase will you use to start your presentation?

What are you going to talk about?

_____
_____
_____

Why is it interesting?

_____
_____
_____

How do you feel about it?

_____
_____

What phrase will you use to close your presentation?

10 | UNIT 1 PART OF THE ART

3 ENGAGING YOUR AUDIENCE IN DIFFERENT WAYS

ORACY 1

Choose 2–3 ways to engage your audience. Write notes.

Ask a question
- _____

Tell an anecdote
- _____

Present a surprising fact
- _____

Use a prop
- _____

Now add these ways to engage to your plan.

Rehearse your presentation. Was it around three minutes? What could you add/cut?

I've decided with my classmate _____ that we'll give each other feedback.

TIP — Collaboration and Teamwork

Be positive when you give feedback to a classmate. For every improvement you suggest, say two things they did well!

After the presentation:
I've spoken with my classmate _____ about her/his presentation, and she/he gave me feedback. I know now that next time I should …

_____
_____

SELF-EVALUATION

I can …
- use my voice effectively. ○
- structure a presentation well. ○
- engage my audience in different ways. ○

UNIT 1 PART OF THE ART | 11

UNIT 2 TELL ME A STORY

VOCABULARY

BOOKS AND STORIES

1 Complete the sentences with adjective + noun collocations from Unit 2.

1. The play has received _____ from the critics.
2. The film-adaptation was an _____. It was a total flop!
3. Sadly, _____ don't always sell many books, even though critics love their writing.
4. The new superhero book series is _____; I can't stop!
5. The incredible true events of her life made a _____.
6. The author's dialogue-free graphic novel was a _____.

2 Complete the sentences with verb + noun collocations about books and stories.

1. My dad is a history teacher, and he's always _____ in the historical series I watch.
2. Would you _____ a book you didn't like to the end, or give up?
3. The audio book didn't _____ enough. I kept getting distracted!
4. That crime fiction podcast really _____ well! I can't wait to know what happens next!
5. I liked the thriller, but the start was slow. It didn't really _____ until chapter 7.
6. What books do teenage boys like? My son needs something to _____ in reading.

READING

✓ EXAM TASK READING AND USE OF ENGLISH PART 5

1 You are going to read an article about storytelling. For questions 1–6, choose the answer (A, B, C or D) which you think fits best according to the text.

1. In the first paragraph, what does the writer say that there is lack of agreement about?
   A why so many different genres of storytelling have thrived
   B what makes certain stories successful
   C how stories have been passed down through the generations
   D whether storytelling developed due to its ability to enhance survival

2. In the second paragraph, the writer suggests that our physical reactions to stories
   A may help us to understand other people's behaviour.
   B are still largely a mystery to scientists.
   C can cause unpleasant sensations.
   D vary from one individual to another.

3. In the third paragraph, it is suggested that people everywhere appreciate stories that
   A show some kind of originality.
   B have a recognisable structure.
   C teach them how to deal with problems.
   D avoid being predictable.

4. In the fourth paragraph, when talking about interesting main characters in stories, the writer is explaining
   A why not everyone can identify with them.
   B their most typical qualities.
   C how they tend to be affected by events.
   D that they need not be good.

5. What point does the writer make about using stories for the purpose of escapism?
   A It is a misguided way for people to deal with difficulties.
   B It enables people to broaden their outlook.
   C It helps people to become more creative.
   D It prevents people from confronting everyday issues.

6. What does the writer suggest about stories in the final paragraph?
   A They should be adaptable.
   B They should provide moral guidance on universal issues.
   C They should be capable of influencing people's moral outlook.
   D They should reflect reality in a dramatic way.

A LOOK INTO THE ART AND SCIENCE OF STORYTELLING

We all love a good story. Whether it's personal anecdotes, folk tales from the Middle East like *One Thousand and One Nights*, action movies or soap operas, stories capture our attention and fire both our imagination and a desire to know more. Some argue they serve an evolutionary purpose. Across millennia, stories, oral and written, have shared information that protected people and enabled greater longevity. For example, the ancient Greek fable of *The Boy Who Cried Wolf* warns about giving false alarms, and lying. In addition, some stories foster social cooperation, as in the ancient Mesopotamian poem, *The Epic of Gilgamesh*, where the relationships depicted illustrate the value of mutual support. Though some say that the idea of an evolutionary basis for storytelling is speculative at best, nobody would disagree that they are powerful tools for communication and persuasion.

There has been great interest in the biological and neurological factors behind our love of stories. Research shows that many regions of the brain are activated when following a story, and brain imaging reveals that neurons in our brains, called mirror neurons, become active in line with the emotions and actions of the characters in a story, allowing us to experience empathy. During a story, our heart rate might increase, we might hold our breath or sigh with relief, and an **absorbing** story can also trigger the hormone oxytocin, creating feelings of connection and trust. Indeed, it seems likely that the brain is built to naturally engage with stories, making us almost **hard-wired** for them.

Studies of well-known stories from around the world indicate that the most popular ones have a beginning, middle and end, much like human life itself, with a narrative that includes elements of conflict, tension and risk of loss or failure. Only once these struggles have been resolved can there be closure. There are no great revelations there, admittedly, though of course much modern experimental literature and filmmaking is at pains to avoid appearing to follow these formulas, which may go some way towards explaining their lack of appeal to the vast majority of people.

In most storylines the protagonist, a central character or hero, provides a driving force. It is their fate that matters to us, and we appreciate the chance to observe human nature in a more intimate way than normal. Sometimes the protagonist is an essentially decent and **virtuous** character, making it easier for the ordinary person to relate to their emotions and the dilemmas they face. Yet, at other times, a more compelling type of protagonist is the villain we find ourselves engaging with against our will. They may be more **nuanced** as characters, or offer a window into our own darker sides, and perhaps encourage us to explore morally grey areas. The most acclaimed works of literature or drama see the protagonist undergo significant development over the course of the story. Their behaviour may provoke questions in us and allow for multiple interpretations.

It is undeniable that storytelling and fiction offer a means for us to be transported out of reality. This kind of distancing of the self from the real world should not be negatively characterised as mere escapism, running away from facing the facts of our real lives. A more positive take on it is that being swept away by a compulsive story and immersing ourselves in an alternative reality, provides something **akin to** a mental vacation, a form of stress-relief, beneficial in moderation, and only a cause for concern if the indulgence is excessive. Above all, escaping from reality offers access to something outside our experience, and a chance to understand other perspectives at a more first-hand level.

Although there is no one-size-fits-all approach for successful storytelling in novels, movies and TV dramas, captivating stories usually involve protagonists coming up against obstacles that must be overcome, such that any human could conceivably identify with their struggle, no matter how far-fetched it is. To become memorable, stylistic techniques such as use of similes and metaphors, **flashbacks**, suspense, or striking camera angles enrich the depiction of characters, events and settings. On top of this, a tale worth recounting ideally has the ability to shift the perspective of its audience concerning what might be right or wrong.

2 Complete the definitions with the words in bold in the text.

1. a short part of a film or story that goes back to events in the past _____
2. slightly different from the norm in appearance, meaning, sound, etc. _____
3. having some similar qualities _____
4. morally good _____
5. interesting and holding attention (like a sponge) _____
6. automatically thinking or behaving in a particular way _____

GRAMMAR

NARRATIVE TENSES

1 Complete the post with the correct form of the verbs in brackets.

> BLOGS ∨   NEWSLETTERS ∨   VIDEOS ∨   🔍
>
> It was last month that I ¹_____ (realise) that campaigns urging us to read more can be bad for us. Why, you may ask? ²_____ (read/I) for hours and hours every day with terrible posture and hurt my back? Yes, but that's not why. Maybe I ³_____ (read) novels when my classmates were studying? That too, but again it isn't the reason they gave. It's actually because we were told to read because it's good for us, and that, I noticed, ⁴_____ (make) me put reading on the list of things I feel guilty about not doing, like going to the gym or the dentist! I ⁵_____ (not/consider) this until I found myself opting out of a night in with a book and going for a 'treat' of a TV series instead. That was not the first time I ⁶_____ (do) that, I'll admit. So, in the end I ⁷_____ (decide) that in future I'll treat my book like a chocolate cake – just one slice (chapter) a night. It's working, because last night was the first time I ⁸_____ (finished) a book for ages, and it made me so pleased! I'm back in the habit again!

2 Choose the correct options to complete the phone call.

A: Hi, are you here at the book signing? I ¹ *expect / expected* to see you, but it's so busy.

B: Sorry! I'm late! I know we planned to ² *meet / meeting* up ... well ... now, and I ³ *am / was* meaning to message you. I'd planned ⁴ *on / to* taking the bus, but had to cycle in the end!

A: No worries. I'm going to get in the queue in the meantime. Let's think about where ⁵ *to meet / meeting* later.

B: Let's meet inside. I ⁶ *'m planning / planned* to get in the queue as soon as I arrive.

USED TO, BE USED TO AND WOULD

3 Choose the correct options to complete the interview extract.

A: As a kid, I ¹ *would / used to* have bedtime story books. How about you? ² *Would / Did* your parents use to read to you?

B: My grandma ³ *would / used*. We ⁴ *would read / were used to reading* the same book in Portuguese practically every night. I ⁵ *would / used to* want her to invent stories too, always about heroic princesses. She made me the main character, and I ⁶ *would / used to* love it. She really helped me become a screenwriter.

A: You wrote stories with her?

B: No, not that, it was more that I ⁷ *would / used to* be shy about telling my own stories, but she made me feel they were great. She built up my confidence.

4 Rewrite the sentences below with *be used to*.

1 Until I got a tablet, reading online felt strange.
2 I read much more in German than English.
3 He always read before bed. It was his routine.
4 Your new glasses will feel normal by next week.
5 I read on my mobile all the time.

5 Read the questions and write short answers about your own life.

1 Are you used to reading books on a digital device or on paper? Why?
2 How often would you go to the library as a kid?
3 What books did you use to borrow?
4 Did you use to read more or less than now?
5 What did you use to like reading, but don't now?

WISH AND IF ONLY

6 Rewrite the sentences using *wish* or *if only*.

1 I regret not buying that book.
2 More time to read would be fantastic!
3 I haven't yet got to the end of the series, and now it isn't available anymore!
4 Oh no! You just told me the ending!
5 I can't remember the name of the film!

7 >>> **STRETCH!** Find and correct eight errors in the text.

Unlike the ancient civilisations in Greece, Syria and China who are used to reading aloud, today we normally read silently. Reading aloud had become something reserved for children, actors, or special occasions. In the past, this ancient art would be help us to improve our memories. We know this because psychologists studying memory found that both children and adults remembered texts better if they were reading them out loud beforehand. They were calling this the 'production effect'. Interestingly, in the study, even mouthing words would made them more memorable to participants. The application of such research can aid everyone learning a new language. If you only you could remember more of what you scribbled into your vocabulary book, but you're used to just look at, not saying, those new words. So, you know what to do – clear your throat and get speaking!

VOCABULARY
ADJECTIVES WITH SUFFIXES

1 Match the two parts of the words to make adjectives with suffixes. You can use the suffixes more than once.

1	feasi	a	-y
2	alarm	b	-ble
3	baby	c	-ed
4	inevit	d	-able
5	length	e	-less
6	price	f	-ish
7	influent	g	-ial
8	frustrat	h	-ic
9	hero		
10	speech		

2 Write another word with each suffix in Exercise 1.

1 _____ y
2 _____ ble
3 _____ ed
4 _____ able
5 _____ less
6 _____ ish
7 _____ ial
8 _____ ic

3 Write a sentence for each of your words above.

READING AND USE OF ENGLISH

☑ **EXAM TASK** — READING AND USE OF ENGLISH PART 3

1 For questions 1–8, read the text below. Use the word given in capitals at the end of some of the lines to form a word that fits in the gap in the same line.

What's behind our love of urban legends?

Heard the story about the guy who ate a particular brand of candy bar, then drank a fizzy soda, and a few minutes later his stomach exploded? This is actually an example of an urban legend, a modern folklore story closely ⁰ __related__ to the phenomenon of false news. Other ¹ _____ examples of the genre are the creepy and ² _____ stories about hitchhikers. Fortunately, these tales have no ³ _____ in real events and are really just cautionary tales of the dangers of hitchhiking. Urban legends do serve a purpose. ⁴ _____, they help us make sense of the world and manage threats in a safe environment, rather like horror films. Urban legends can be a ⁵ _____ form of entertainment. They often have an element of ⁶ _____, leading to a shocking ending. Whether by word of mouth or online messaging, passing on such stories is a form of social ⁷ _____. The person doing it feels as if they are sharing valuable information, even though an internet check would quickly reveal the lack of ⁸ _____ evidence behind the story.

RELATE
COMPEL
FORGET
BASE
PSYCHOLOGY
GRIP
ENGAGE
FACT

UNIT 2 TELL ME A STORY | 15

EXAM TIP

Before reading the options, read the two task questions so you have a general idea of what the speakers will talk about.

LISTENING

1 What was the last piece of creative writing you did? Who read it? How did their feedback make you feel?

✓ EXAM TASK   LISTENING PART 4

2 🔊 2.1 You will hear five short extracts in which people are talking about a creative writing course they attended. While you listen, you must complete both tasks.

TASK ONE

For questions **1–5**, choose from the list **(A–H)** what each speaker says was their main reason for attending the creative writing course.

A to fulfil a long-held intention
B to get professional feedback
C to develop new writing techniques
D to experience a sense of challenge
E to make writing a regular habit
F to gain confidence in their writing
G to meet other literature enthusiasts
H to engage in an enjoyable activity

Speaker 1 [1]
Speaker 2 [2]
Speaker 3 [3]
Speaker 4 [4]
Speaker 5 [5]

TASK TWO

For Questions **6–10**, choose from the list **(A–H)** how each speaker felt during the course.

A frustrated by the style of teaching
B surprised by how committed other students were
C proud of the amount of progress made
D grateful to receive plenty of encouragement
E relieved that others had similar levels of ability
F alarmed by how much work was required
G enthusiastic about writing as a possible career
H anxious about commenting on the work of others

Speaker 1 [6]
Speaker 2 [7]
Speaker 3 [8]
Speaker 4 [9]
Speaker 5 [10]

3 Read the extracts from the listening. Match the words and phrases in bold to their meaning a–e.

1 I've **dabbled** in creative writing over the years
2 ... it wasn't **up to scratch**
3 Most people were **in the same boat**, coming after a long day's work
4 ... it was more stressful than I'd **anticipated**.
5 ... it was run by several **acclaimed** authors ...

a in the same, usually difficult, circumstances
b praised by many people
c to do something in a casual way, or as a hobby
d at the required standard
e to have imagined or expected something

4 💼 **Professional Development and Management**
Write answers to the questions.

1 Do you think creative writing is a useful skill to have? Why? / Why not?
2 Do you think there's a high demand for good writers in the job market? In which industry is it highest?
2 What could you do to further develop your creative writing skills?

WRITING

AN ESSAY

1 Read the exam task below. Then read the model answer and underline four phrases that show the writer's opinion.

EXAM TIP

Use your own words. Paraphrase the language used in the exam notes for the introduction, reasons and opinions.

EXAM TASK — WRITING PART 1

Your class has watched a documentary about why people are reading fewer novels these days. You have made the notes below:

reasons people are reading fewer novels
- availability of online movies and series
- lack of access to books
- modern lifestyles

Some opinions expressed in the documentary:

'Streaming services offer so many great movies and TV series online.'

'Novels are expensive and there are no libraries in my area.'

'I'm always busy reading stuff on social media so I don't have time to read novels.'

Write an essay discussing two of the points in the notes. You should explain why you think people are reading fewer novels these days, giving reasons to support your opinion. You may, if you wish, make use of the opinions expressed in the documentary, but you should use your own words as far as possible.
Write your answer in 220–260 words.

2 Make notes for each point below.
1. Introduction
2. Discuss one of the points, giving your opinion
3. Discuss another point, giving your opinion
4. Conclusion showing which point you think is more important

---

The documentary I watched explored the reasons behind the decline in novel reading, attributing it primarily to the availability of online movies and dramas and the demands of modern lifestyles. Both factors have significantly contributed to this trend, yet I believe the influence of streaming services is the more important factor.

Streaming services offer a huge number of high-quality movies and TV dramas that cater to a wide range of tastes and preferences. These platforms also provide 24-hour entertainment, both of which mean people can become immediately engaged with content, unlike the slower process of reading a novel. With the rise of binge-watching culture, people have become immersed in the continuous storylines offered by series, a format which people find less arduous than reading.

On the other hand, it cannot be denied that modern lifestyles are also characterized by people feeling constantly busy and having continuous connectivity to online social media. It seems to me that the presence of digital distractions leaves little time or mental space for the focused concentration that novels require. However, this can be seen as a secondary effect of the broader digital entertainment systems, in which streaming services play a central part.

On balance, while both factors are significant, the attraction of streaming services seems to be the primary reason for the decline in reading novels. Their ability to provide instant, visually compelling entertainment has made them a more tempting alternative to traditional reading.

3 Write your essay. Use 220–260 words.

SELF-EVALUATION

Check your writing:

Content: Have you covered the two points in a balanced way? Have you given reasons and offered explanations? ☹ ☺ 😐 😊

Communication: Is your opinion clear to the reader? ☹ ☺ 😐 😊

Organisation: Is the text well-organised and linked? Is there a good flow of ideas? ☹ ☺ 😐 😊

Language: Have you used a variety of structures and vocabulary? Have you included some new language from this unit? ☹ ☺ 😐 😊

URBAN CANVASES

1 GETTING STARTED

My partner is: _____

Do you and your partner agree with Ben Eine?
_____

2 THINK

I'm working with: _____

Three pieces of art we know that can help discussion around social or environmental issues:

1 _____
2 _____
3 _____

Do any of these include underrepresented voices? Whose voices?

3 EXPLORE

What?
_____

How effective?
_____

What artist?
_____

Street art projects in our area
_____

What's the message?
_____

Where?
_____

Who for?
_____

TIP Start by talking as a group about street art you've seen in your town. Then, search for examples online (you might need to do this in your L1). If you can't find anything about your town, try a bigger town or nearby city.

18 | UNIT 2 TELL ME A STORY

4 DEVELOP

EXPLORING SUSTAINABILITY 1

Introduction: The example of street art we're going to present is …
You can see …
Question for the audience?

_____
_____
_____

Body:
Effective message?
Broaden discussions?
Anything else?

Plan

_____
_____
_____

Ending:
This piece of street art is important because …

Have you looked back at the oracy task in Unit 1 to help you plan an effective presentation?

Use your notes from Stage 3 here.

TIP — **Collaboration and Teamwork**
Think about how you will show the street art to your audience. When you show it, could you ask a question about it to engage them?

Collaboration and Teamwork
Does everyone know what they're doing?
Do we know which order we're presenting in?
Have we got everything we need for the presentation?

5 PRESENT

Reflections on the discussion
Things we did well:

_____
_____
_____
_____

Things we could improve:

_____
_____
_____
_____

SELF-EVALUATION

I can …
- identify and explain street art which relates to social or environmental issues. ○
- identify, gather and organise relevant information. ○
- broaden discussions to include underrepresented voices. ○
- work constructively in a group presentation. ○

UNIT 3 OTHER SIDE OF THE COIN

VOCABULARY

PERSONAL FINANCE

1 Complete the phrases with the words from the box. Some words can be used more than once.

> account borrow debit get into
> income market payment transfer
> savings shares spend withdraw

Verb phrases

1 _____ heavily
2 _____ debt
3 _____ a fortune
4 _____ cash

Noun phrases

5 contactless _____
6 a current _____
7 direct _____
8 electronic _____
9 life _____
10 source of _____
11 stock _____
12 stocks and _____

2 Complete the text with phrases from Exercise 1.

A news story went viral last week about a new ATM for dogs. The article claimed our four-legged friends could perform a function akin to ¹_____ on it, but instead of money the machine would give out tasty treats. They would do this with just a tap of the paw, like a type of ²_____. The machine was said to be linked to the owners' ³_____, which would be charged for the treats at the end of each month.

It went on to say that dog owners could also load the account with treats using instant ⁴_____ each time they left for the park, or even set up a ⁵_____ to ensure enough snacks for man's best friend. Cheaply priced, owners would not have to ⁶_____ to keep their pets happy.

The article finished by saying that to invest, readers could enquire about buying ⁷_____ in the company. The email address given was dogatm@jokearticle.com, and while many readers realised they'd been fooled, some reportedly sent emails. Don't believe everything you read online!

READING

EXAM TIP

Don't spend time reading the text without knowing what you're searching for. Read each question carefully before scanning the text to find the information you need.

✓ EXAM TASK READING AND USE OF ENGLISH PART 6

1 You are going to read four extracts from articles about the links between money and happiness. For questions 1–4, choose from the extracts A–D. The extracts may be chosen more than once.

Which writer

has a different view from the others about how making wealth a key goal affects happiness? [1]

shares reviewer C's opinion about how different income groups value a sense of purpose in their lives? [2]

has a different view from reviewer B on how informative research into wealth and happiness is? [3]

expresses a similar opinion to reviewer A regarding the happiness of the richest in society? [4]

Money and Happiness

FOUR WRITERS GIVE THEIR VIEWS

A Many studies have been done on the subject of money and happiness, with new studies coming out on a regular basis. Concepts like happiness are hard to define, but these studies generally talk about the relationship between how rich we are and our emotional welfare and life satisfaction; basically how good or bad we feel both in the moment and about our life circumstances overall. It comes as no surprise that prioritising the quest for money has been shown to impair enjoyment of life and **dampen** overall satisfaction. Personal responsibilities, for example bringing up children, help give life significance, and such commitments make life as meaningful for those with little money as for someone with plenty. Interestingly, the ultra-wealthy people I've met all seemed rather pessimistic and **grumpy**, despite being free to spend a fortune on buying the best of whatever they desire at any moment.

B The numerous studies conducted have added greatly to our understanding of how money impacts on people's levels of contentment and satisfaction. It was good to have confirmed what I have long thought to be true, which is that people who are focused on financial success as an ambition report taking less pleasure in family life, friendships, and their work than those whose **lives revolve around** other issues. It's also been shown that moderately wealthy people are generally happy, in conditions where there is only moderate inequality between income levels. Of course, it's obviously easier to follow your interests, provide for your family and live well if you have more money, and these things are partly what provide meaning for people. However, the super-rich appear to be mostly obsessed with making more and more money and are, consequently, miserable. At least that's what I've observed from personal experience.

C I would assert that feelings of positivity and satisfaction are equally important to all humans. Furthermore, these feelings are strongly associated with viewing life with a sense of purpose, importance and direction. This surely matters to people at all levels of society, from the richest to the poorest. Although it generally benefits your sense of well-being to **have money rolling in**, it can have toxic results if its pursuit is your primary motivation. According to many studies, even multi-millionaires aren't significantly happier than those working with regular amounts of money. It's all about having enough, and once you exceed the point at which you have a comfortable life where you aren't constantly worrying about money, going up a few income levels seems to have little effect.

D Various studies have confirmed the idea that having more money can improve your well-being. Without wishing to offend those who make it their business to investigate these matters, some of their findings do appear somewhat obvious. I don't think anyone believes that the sports cars and private jets that multi-millionaires cruise around in are crucial to happiness, but we all know that a home and financial security are. You can't even begin to think about having a meaningful life or achieving life satisfaction without such things. I'm also dismissive of the **notion** that the more you aim at financial success, the less content you will be. After all, if having money boosts happiness, then surely you need to be motivated to obtain it. Those who have to borrow heavily to do anything beyond survive, or are constantly getting into debt, have consistently higher anxiety levels than those who are comfortably off.

2 Complete the sentences with the correct form of the words and phrases in bold in the article.

1 At the moment my _____ schoolwork, so I'm looking forward to the holidays!
2 The new company is doing really well, they _____!
3 The bad weather report _____ our enthusiasm for the camping trip.
4 The activist group rejects the _____ that banks are interested in sustainability.
5 Being stuck in traffic for hours made everyone _____. They argued over tiny things.

GRAMMAR

MODAL VERBS – REVIEW

1 Complete the table with the modals from the box.

> can   can't   have to   don't have to
> must   mustn't   should   shouldn't

1 There is a consequence:	_____ _____ _____
2 It is advisable:	_____ _____
3 There isn't a consequence:	_____ _____

2 Complete the text with modals of obligation. What object is being described?

I think every child ¹_____ have one of these. I did when I was young! I remember how it works. You ²_____ to do jobs around the house to help your parents, and they give you coins. The rule is that you ³_____ spend them; you save them by putting them in the hole. I loved the sound of the coins dropping! It ⁴_____ be in the shape of a pig, it could be anything! You ⁵_____ get the money out because there is only a hole in the top, so basically, you're saving it. The important thing to tell the child is that there is a rule, and it's that they absolutely ⁶_____ break it open until it's full, or it's bad luck. Did you have one?

MODAL VERBS IN THE PAST

3 Complete the conversation using the past modal verbs in the box.

> couldn't   didn't have to   had to   needed to
> should have   weren't able to

A: Why are you home so late?
B: What a rubbish evening! My bank card didn't work at the station ticket machine so I ¹_____ walk home.
A: You ²_____ called me!
B: My mobile died too, so I ³_____ even do that.
A: So you ⁴_____ get the stuff we needed for dinner, then?
B: What? I ²_____ get food for dinner? I thought I ⁶_____ because you were doing it! This is the worst day ever.

4 Write answers to the questions.
1 Were you able to save money when you were younger?
2 As a kid, could you spend money on anything you wanted?
3 Were you able to earn pocket money from doing housework?

5 Complete the text with a past modal form of the verbs in brackets.

HOME   ARTICLES

Cowrie shells were an early way to pay for goods, particularly in Africa and parts of Asia. Archaeologists are certain that they ¹_____ (serve) as a currency from patterns of shells found in ancient burial sites and trade centres. It's said that people in China ²_____ (can) use cowrie shells for various transactions, from buying goods to settling debts, from the 4th century BC onwards. The shells then spread from Asia to as far as West Africa, which must have been due to travelling traders. These ³_____ (not be) easy journeys, but the quest to be a millionaire existed even back then. But why cowrie shells? They ⁴_____ (be) chosen because of their rarity and beauty, but this is only speculation. It's also thought that societies ⁵_____ (have) develop methods to ensure the shells were authentic, because counterfeit shells were also found. Of course, even then people ⁶_____ (allow) to pay with fake currency, but this shows they attempted to. So, while not proven, the use of cowrie shells ⁷_____ (shape) the development of today's currency in significant ways.

6 STRETCH! Complete the second sentence so that is has a similar meaning to the first sentence, using the word given. Do not change the word given. Use between three and four words.

1 Perhaps I left my wallet at yours. **MIGHT**
   I _____ to pick up my wallet from yours.

2 I didn't manage to save any money last year. **ABLE**
   I _____ save any money last year.

READING AND USE OF ENGLISH

✓ EXAM TASK READING AND USE OF ENGLISH PART 2

1 For questions 1–8, read the text below and think of the word which best fits each gap. Use only one word in each gap. There is an example at the beginning (0).

THE CASHLESS SOCIETY

The world has witnessed a major shift in ⁰ _how_ people pay for goods and services. ¹_____ was once the case that cash in the form of coins and notes served ²_____ the primary method of making transactions. People might also ³_____ had to queue in a banks to cash a cheque.

Today, electronic transfers and direct debits have transformed our finances. Societies everywhere are increasingly moving towards solely digital transactions, all of ⁴_____ has been facilitated by rapid technological advances. The use of smartphone apps to make payments offers convenience for both buyer and seller, while online banking apps provide individuals ⁵_____ instant access to their accounts in a way that was once unimaginable.

In ⁶_____ of efforts to assist people with adapting to a cashless economy, some still struggle to keep ⁷_____ with these developments. And a few decades into the future, the pace of technological change suggests the young of today ⁸_____ well find themselves in similar situations.

VOCABULARY
PHRASAL VERBS

1 Complete the phrasal verbs with the correct preposition.

1 bail someone _____
2 dip _____ savings
3 come _____ money
4 pay _____ a pension
5 put _____ a deposit
6 rent _____ property
7 rip someone _____
8 money roll(s) _____
9 run _____ money
10 work _____ debt

2 Complete the text with the correct form of a phrasal verb from Exercise 1.

BLOGS | CONTACT Search...

When you think about it, the popular board game Monopoly is quite peculiar. Players often find themselves in situations where they must say no to ¹_____ a friend from jail or decide to ²_____ at an unaffordable rate to a family member. The game can quickly turn ugly if someone gets lucky and ³_____, leaving others to fall into poverty. Feeling annoyed as you're being ⁴_____ by a loved one isn't a great way to spend a Sunday evening. Many don't enjoy playing for this reason. In its defence, what the game may teach us is strategies for life like ⁵_____ only when needed and ⁶_____ on properties whenever you can afford to. It can show us what life is like when money isn't ⁷_____. Do you love it or loathe it?

UNIT 3 OTHER SIDE OF THE COIN | 23

LISTENING

1 Look at the items below. Which of them would you prefer to recieve as a birthday present? Why?

concert tickets

photos

clothes

video games

a notebook

a meal

2 🔊 3.1 Listen to a conversation. Why are each of the presents in Exercise 1 mentioned? Make notes.

3 🔊 3.1 Listen again. Decide if the sentences are true, false or the information is not given.
   1 The Get Back Boys are a new group.
   2 Alex is confident he knows what his mum would like.
   3 The present that Alex got his dad cost a lot.
   4 Alex's Dad is going to get Alex an experience-based present too.
   5 Alex's dad has tried the restaurant in the city centre.

4 🔊 3.1 Alex's dad's attitude to experience-based gifts changes during the discussion. Listen again and match his attitude with the language he uses to express it. Some attitudes have more than one correct answer.
   1 he's completely sceptical
   2 he starts to get interested
   3 he becomes enthusiastic
   4 he's convinced

   a point taken, and challenge accepted
   b that just won't do
   c go on
   d That isn't a ...
   e I'm going to go for ...
   f I get what you're saying

5 Write two or three sentences to summarise what the conversation says about presents.

6 **Innovation and Problem Solving** Alex thinks that experiences make better presents. Think of some reasons why people might not enjoy this type of present and write an email to Alex to try and persuade him to change his mind.

24   UNIT 3 OTHER SIDE OF THE COIN

WRITING

A REPORT

1 Read the exam task. Complete the table with the phrases in the box.

> a way of making people interested in
> to some extent   companies could promote
> a great deal   not enough as they should
> one method to push people towards

Phrases to answer the first question:	
Phrases to answer the second question:	

EXAM TIP

A report will always ask for a recommendation, so make sure you know the structure of common verbs to do this.

2 Read the extracts of recommendations from a report. Which are appropriate? Which are not appropriate? Why?

1. For this reason, I strongly urge local councils to take action and …
2. It is due to the various reasons above that I suggest …
3. Some people think that this is the best solution, yet others have a different view.
4. … and with these changes, a difference could surely be made.
5. As mentioned above, many changes are needed. It is now the government's job to decide how.

3 Read the exam task again and plan your review. Make notes for each paragraph.

1. Introduction (e.g. purpose of the report, what country, what topic, why the topic is important)

2. What environmental factors are there? Do these influence people in my country?

3. Encouraging more environmentally friendly buying

4. Closing sentence/recommendation

EXAM TASK — WRITING PART 2

Leadership and Global Citizenship

An international research group is investigating how environmental factors affect people's attitudes to buying things in shops and online. You have been asked to write a report on people's attitudes in your country.

Your report should address the following questions:

How much do environmental factors influence people in your country when buying things in shops and online?

How could people be encouraged to be more environmentally friendly in their buying choices?

4 Write your report. Write your answer in 220–260 words.

SELF-EVALUATION

Check your writing:

Content: Have you answered both the questions? Have you written about buying both in shops and online?

Communication: Can the reader clearly see what you think are the best buying choices? Is the style appropriate for a report?

Organisation: Have you included a title and headings? Is the text well-organised and linked? ☹ ☺ 😐 😊

Language: Have you used a variety of structures and vocabulary? Have you included some new language from this unit?

UNIT 3 OTHER SIDE OF THE COIN | 25

NEGOTIATING

1 PLANNING/BRAINSTORMING

Facilitating a positive environment

At the moment our outdoor area at school is:
_____

Five things we could spend money on:
_____
_____
_____
_____
_____

Two things I most want to spend money on, and my reasons why:
_____
_____
_____
_____

Phrases I could use to interrupt if I don't agree with something.

TIP Disagreement doesn't have to mean conflict! Express your disagreement politely and respectfully.

2 IDENTIFYING STRONG AND WEAKER ARGUMENTS

What questions will you ask to find out why someone believes something?

Someone else might want to spend money on … because …
_____
_____

Why I find this argument weak:
_____
_____

UNIT 3 OTHER SIDE OF THE COIN

3 PERSUADING

ORACY 2

💼 Collaboration and Teamwork

Persuading strategies I want to use (tick two!):

- ☐ Asking someone to think about something, e.g. (*What can you say?*) ...
- ☐ Helping them to understand my idea e.g.
- ☐ Offering evidence for my idea e.g.
- ☐ Using more precise language e.g.

write examples

Now add some persuasive language to your reasons why.

After the negotiation:

How did your group decide to use the money?

_____
_____

After the presentation:

I've spoken with my classmate _____ about her/his presentation, and she/he gave me feedback. I know now that next time I should ...

_____
_____
_____

TIP Recording your conversation and reviewing it afterwards can help you come up with better feedback.

SELF-EVALUATION

I can ...

- facilitate a positive environment during a negotiation. ○
- identify strong and weak arguments. ○
- use language for persuading. ○

REVIEW 1 UNITS 1–3

GRAMMAR 1

1 Choose the correct options to complete the text.

I ¹ *wish / 'm wishing* my sister was more private on social media. She ² *takes / is taking* so many photos of us, and she ³ *constantly is posting / is constantly posting* what we're doing. Something's happened today and I ⁴ *'m / 'm being* a bit angry at her. She posted a photo of us at an art gallery with my friend Jo and I ⁵ *guarantee / 'm guaranteeing* you my other friend Robbi will get annoyed with me because I didn't invite her. I mean, she never actually ⁷ *enjoys / is enjoying* going to art galleries, but she ⁸ *doesn't want / isn't wanting* to feel left out of the group either. I'm ⁹ *really hoping / hoping really* that she doesn't feel bad because I ¹⁰ *understand / 'm understanding* her completely. I just wish my sister hadn't posted anything! Grrr!

2 Complete the sentences with the present perfect simple or continuous and the verb in brackets.

1 I _____ (always / be) fascinated by photography.
2 Recently I _____ (learn), little by little, how to use an analogue camera.
3 The camera _____ (be) in our attic for years, so my mum said I could have it.
4 Every night this week she _____ (teach) me how to use it. I'm getting better every day!
5 I _____ (make) tutorial videos on my mobile to help a friend use his own old camera.
6 When you finish a roll of film, you send it to an online company. When they _____ (develop) and printed the photos, they send them back.
7 Once you _____ (use) an analogue camera, you won't go back to digital!
8 I _____ (try) to find another old camera to buy when I have a bit more money.

VOCABULARY 1

1 Complete the text with phrases from the box. You do not need to use all of the phrases.

> art enthusiast   family gathering   flying visit
> keen participant   hilarious comedy
> perfect venue   quality time   social whirl
> total flop   unforgettable experience

For their 50th wedding anniversary, my grandparents planned a big ¹ _____ in a hotel in Málaga with all my aunts, uncles and cousins. They spent their honeymoon there in the 70s so it was the ² _____. The best part of the trip was of course the ³ _____ we spent together as a family (particularly the one-day ⁴ _____ from my cousin who lives in Seville). I hadn't seen her for years! Another highlight for me was the Picasso Museum. As a(n) ⁵ _____ I'd always wanted to go there and my dream finally came true. Another great evening was our theatre trip. We saw a(n) ⁶ _____. Even my serious uncle couldn't stop laughing. My only regret from the weekend was that we didn't get a decent group photo. We did try, but the attempt was a(n) ⁷ _____ because no one could stop laughing! Last weekend really was a(n) ⁸ _____.

2 Complete the conversation with the correct adjective. Use the first letter to help you.

Adi: So, what did you think of the film?
Sonny: Well, I found it ¹ g_____ in parts, especially the beginning. But as it went on, the story felt a bit ² d_____. I didn't understand the connection between the characters.
Adi: Totally! Some of the plot twists were very ³ f_____. I mean, how could he have escaped that prison?
Sonny: And the ending was supposed to be ⁴ m_____, but the actors were ⁵ u_____ to me. I don't think anyone would cry at that.
Adi: It was supposed to be ⁶ h_____, and sad, but it felt so ⁷ h_____. I've seen that kind of ending a million times. Everyone's calling the film ⁸ g_____ because of the new AI graphics, but it wasn't the five stars I expected. It's so ⁹ o_____.

GRAMMAR 2

1 Complete the conversation with the verbs in the box in the correct form.

> be follow like move not notice
> realise sit try understand watch

Jia: So, how was the English homework challenge last night?

Raj: Not bad! I watched a film called *Police Chase*. I really ¹_____ the actors; they were very funny. I ²_____ on the sofa when my mum walked in and asked me to put subtitles on. I looked at her, confused, because I ³_____ they weren't! To my surprise I saw that I ⁴_____ it in English and following everything. That was only the second time I ⁵_____ a film in English without subtitles. The other time ⁶_____ in my English class!

Jia: Wow, good for you. Last night was the first time I ⁷_____ putting *The Wedding* on in English, but in the end, I changed to French. I was getting it when suddenly the action ⁸_____ from California to Manchester, and I don't understand that accent. In fact, I thought I ⁹_____ all the story in California, but when I changed to French I ¹⁰_____ I'd completely misunderstood some parts. At least I tried!

2 Correct the errors in the sentences.

1. He used be a teacher. Then he became an actor!
2. What books would you reading over and over as a child?
3. I'm not used to read in a car, I feel sick!
4. At primary school, did you used to write your own stories?

3 Rewrite the sentences using *wish* or *if only*.

1. Being at creative writing camp would be so good!
2. I'd rather not be here at summer school.
3. Imagine talking about stories all day; it would be awesome.
4. I should have studied more for my exams.
5. Watching the film before I read the end of the book was a bad idea!

VOCABULARY 2

1 Complete the text with the words in the box.

> acclaimed attention compelling compulsive
> glowing holes interest suspense through

Last week, Bonnytown high school hosted a talk with a(n) ¹_____ author whose latest novel has received ²_____ reviews. Over 200 students came to the event; fans of the ³_____ story about a fantasy world. What started as simple social media posts quickly became ⁴_____ reading for many, which eventually led to a full novel. Much of the novel's success is attributed to how the author held her readers' ⁵_____ with those initial posts. Publishing one part of a story every day built up ⁶_____ and gave her regular followers on social media. This, plus the fact the novel has only 300 pages, has helped her succeed. Fans say they would not wade ⁷_____ a 500-page fantasy novel but can manage this. Although some critics have picked ⁸_____ in her simple writing style, she seems to have awakened many teens' ⁹_____ in literature.

2 Complete the text with the correct suffixes. There are two suffixes you do not need to use.

> -able -ed (x2) -ible -ic
> -ish -less (x2) -tial -y

Want to get back into reading but can't? Throw away the idea that reading for pleasure is only ¹ feas_____ for people with lots of free time and check out graphic novels! My cousin introduced me to them, and my parents are ² speech_____ by how quickly I got back into reading. Like you, I admit I was initially ³ alarm_____ by the ⁴ length_____ novels on the bookshop shelves, and felt ⁵ frustrat_____ that I couldn't find much for my age. That first book he gave me changed everything; it was really ⁶ influen_____ to me. I had thought graphic novels would be ⁷ baby_____ but they weren't at all. What I will say is that finding the right book for you is a ⁸ price_____ moment. Once you've found that, returning to reading is easy!

REVIEW 1 | 29

REVIEW 1 UNITS 1–3

GRAMMAR 3

1 Choose the correct options to complete the text.

As a teenager, getting weekly pocket money can give you a sense of freedom, because you ¹ *don't have to / have to* ask your parents every time you ² *need to / can* buy something. However, you ³ *mustn't / must* forget that this money isn't endless, meaning you ⁴ *don't have to / should* think carefully before you spend it. It ⁵ *might / should* be tempting to spend it all in one day, but you ⁶ *ought to / must* save some for later. One day you ⁷ *must / could* be stuck and ⁸ *should / need* extra then!

2 Complete the conversation with the past modals in the box.

> need to   should have   was able to
> was allowed to   were you able
> would have   would have to

Ben: So, ¹ _____ to get a present for your basketball coach?

Mo: We were, yeah! We all put money in and told people that no-one ² _____ say anything to her, so I think it's still a secret.

Ben: You ³ _____ told me, I ⁴ _____ given you something.

Mo: Aw, thanks, but we've got it now!

Ben: Cool. How many people did you ⁵ _____ ask before you had enough money?

Mo: Well, I had calculated that everyone in the team ⁶ _____ put in £3 each. But so many people gave more than that, in the end I ⁷ _____ buy the gift and some flowers!

SELF-ASSESSMENT!

3 Look back at your work in Units 1–3.

- ☐ present simple and present continuous
- ☐ present perfect
- ☐ narrative tenses
- ☐ *used to*, *be used to* and *would*
- ☐ *wish* and *if only*
- ☐ modal verbs – review
- ☐ modal verbs in the past

1 Tick ✓ the area of grammar that you feel most confident about.
2 ⓒircle the area of grammar that you need to work on more.
3 Underline the area of grammar that you think you will use most in future.

VOCABULARY 3

1 Complete the text with words related to personal finance.

Are you getting into ¹ d_____ and need to spend less? Make smarter choices in how you spend and save. For instance, instead of ² w_____ cash and not knowing what you spent it on, go electronic. Contactless ³ p_____ and direct ⁴ d_____ to pay bills helps you track your spending better. Many people find they stop spending a ⁵ f_____ on lunch and coffees when they see how much it adds up to. You could also have a separate ⁶ c_____ account called 'weekly spending' and a savings account. Do an electronic ⁷ t_____ to divide the money into these two accounts. Then, when you have enough savings, put them into stocks and ⁸ s_____.

2 Complete the sentences with the correct form of the phrases in the box. There are two extra you do not need to use.

> bail someone out   dip into savings
> put down a deposit   rent out property
> run through the money   work off debt

1 After unexpectedly losing his job, Mark had to _____ to cover his mortgage payments.
2 Before moving into their new apartment, they had to _____ of £5,000.
3 Sarah inherited a large sum of money, but she managed to _____ within a year due to her extravagant lifestyle.
4 Many homeowners choose to _____ as an extra source of income.

SELF-ASSESSMENT!

3 Look back at your work in Units Units 1–3.

- ☐ leisure collocations
- ☐ arts adjectives
- ☐ books and stories
- ☐ adjectives with suffixes
- ☐ personal finance
- ☐ phrasal verbs

1 Tick ✓ the vocabulary group that had the most new words for you.
2 ⓒircle the vocabulary group that you need to work on more.
3 Underline the vocabulary group that you think you will use most in future.

VOCABULARY REFERENCE 1-3

UNIT 1

art enthusiast a person who loves art
family gathering a party or meeting of many people from one family
flying visit a very short trip to see someone or something
keen participant someone who enjoys taking part in an activity
hilarious comedy a film that makes you laugh a lot
perfect venue an ideal place to hold an event
quality time relaxing activities where people slow down and appreciate each other
social whirl a time or lifestyle full of parties and social activities
total flop a completely unsuccessful film, book, etc.
unforgettable experience something you did or saw which you will always remember
disjointed not well organised or well connected
far-fetched exaggerated and hard to believe
gripping extremely interesting or exciting
groundbreaking completely new and different
hackneyed used or said too often
harrowing very upsetting
moving making you feel an emotional response
overrated considered to be better than it really is
tedious very boring
unconvincing not seeming to be real or true

UNIT 2

acclaimed author a writer who is widely praised
bold experiment an innovative attempt
compelling story a narrative that is very interesting and readers can't stop reading
compulsive reading a book so fascinating that it's hard to stop reading
glowing reviews extremely positive feedback
unmitigated disaster when something is a total failure
awaken someone's interest help someone become interested in something
build up the suspense make a plot more and more gripping
hold someone's attention keep someone interested
fire someone's imagination help someone have original, exciting ideas
pick holes in something find problems with something
wade through something finish reading something even though you aren't enjoying it
alarmed worried that something bad might happen
babyish behaving like a child in an immature way
feasible possible to do or achieve
frustrated feeling annoyed because something is not going as planned
heroic showing great courage or bravery
influential having the power to change something
inevitable certain to happen and cannot be avoided
lengthy continuing for a long time
priceless extremely valuable or important
speechless unable to speak because of shock or amazement

UNIT 3

contactless payment paying by holding your card or phone over a small machine
current account a bank account
direct debit paying by letting an organisation take money directly from your account
electronic transfer sending money digitally from your bank account to another one
get into debt get a lot of money from the bank, which you have to pay back
life savings all the money you have saved in your life
source of income a job, an investment, or anything that provides you with money
spend a fortune pay a huge amount of money for one or many things
spend heavily spend more than you have
stock market where investors buy and sell parts of the ownership of companies
stocks and shares parts of the ownership of a company, which people can buy and sell
withdraw/spend cash take some money out of your bank account, usually using your card and a machine
dip into savings spend a small part of some money
work off debt get rid of something through activity
pay into a pension regularly put money into some kind of fund
bail someone out rescue a person or organisation in financial difficulties
come into money get money because a relative has died
rip someone off charge too much money
rent out property get money for the use of property
money rolls in arrive in large amounts
pay a deposit pay a first part of the cost of something
run through money use a lot of something

DIGITAL CLASSROOM
PRACTICE EXTRA UNITS 1-3

UNIT 4 YOU LIVE, YOU LEARN

VOCABULARY
STUDY AND EXAMS

1 Read the definitions and write the phrases from Unit 4.

1 money that a student borrows from a bank to pay for their education _____

2 exams taken at the end of a university course _____

3 a piece of work or job that you are given to do on a course _____

4 using another person's idea or work and pretending it is your own _____

5 the money that you pay to study on a course _____

6 the money given to a person by an organisation to pay for their education _____

7 a time by which something must be done _____

8 a university student on a degree course _____

9 the months when you attend school or university _____

10 a plan showing the order of topics and/or books to be studied in a course _____

11 a visit made by students to study something away from a school or university _____

12 a very long piece of writing done as part of a course _____

2 Complete the blog with words from Exercise 1.

Are STANDARDIZED EXAMS really the best way to assess learning?
We ask university students their opinions

Hi all, I'm a second-year student, and happy to share my experiences. You might not know this, but throughout the ¹_____, we're expected to complete a variety of ²_____ like group work and presentations with other ³_____, as well as participate in activities like ⁴_____. In my uni, we were told all this on the first day, when our tutor gave out the ⁵_____ to us. That also had the reading list and all the exam dates on it. Depending on your course, the ⁶_____ at the end can be worth up to 70% of your grade, and the pressure to perform on those tests can be so huge that it affects some people's health. That's one reason I don't think they're the best way to evaluate us. On top of that, the stress of these exams can also affect some students' performance, which puts their access to ⁷_____ at risk as grades can influence those decisions. Some of my friends rely on that financial help as they can't afford to pay their own ⁸_____. I realise we need to get tested at the end of the year, but I think I'd rather be assessed on my course work, or even on one long project a year, kind of like the ⁹_____ you do at the very end of your degree. I've learned so much from my first year, but not only from exams. I'm learning how to communicate well, how to reference ideas in my essays so as to not be guilty of ¹⁰_____, how to manage my time to deal with strict ¹¹_____, and things like that. I'm also learning to budget so I don't spend my ¹²_____ too quickly! What I'm saying is that standardised exams aren't everything. Do you agree?

3 >>> STRETCH! Cross out the verb that does not collocate with the noun.

1 *make / go on / organise / attend* a field trip
2 *hand in / repeat / sit / write* an assignment
3 *follow / cover / read / retake* a syllabus
4 *resit / take / make / retake* finals
5 *commit / do / detect / avoid* plagiarism
6 *fail / meet / make / have* a deadline

READING

1 Read the application email. Which course is Kim applying for?

a astrobiology
b domestic science
c folklore
d zoology

Inbox — 4 Messages

Subject: Course application

Dear Professor Dern,

I am writing to express my strong interest in opting for the ………?……… class that you are teaching next academic year. Although I am majoring in geography, one of my personal passions is reading up on the origins of life. I am eager to expand my knowledge and contribute to this fascinating field.

My interest in the class has been fuelled by a presentation assignment I did on the environmental conditions of extraterrestrial bodies. I believe that through this course I may gain the knowledge I need to plan my dissertation on this topic. I would like to present this dissertation for my degree in the social sciences department, but also for it to be a piece of work that might help me to gain entrance into a masters in your department.

As I mention above, I am currently a social sciences undergraduate, yet my high school grades and previous college diploma go some way towards proving that I also have a solid foundation in biology and chemistry, which I think would serve me well in your class. If needed, my lecturer from my food chemistry class in college could act as a referee. Is there a departmental email address he could send this to?

I am confident that my academic background and enthusiasm for your subject will allow me to contribute meaningfully to the course. I understand that only science undergraduates are normally admitted onto your course, but I hope that an exception might be made in this instance.

Please find my attached grade record for your consideration. I am happy to provide any additional information or documentation if required.

Thank you in advance for taking the time to read my email. I hope to hear from you soon.

Yours sincerely,

Kim Shek

---

2 Read the email again. Answer the questions in your own words.

1 What knowledge does Kim already have in this field?
2 What's Kim's hope for the future?
3 How could a previous lecturer help her?
4 Why might Kim not be given a place?

3 Find words or phrases in the email which mean:

1 choosing
2 finding information about something
3 good basis
4 help me
5 given a place
6 for you to look at

4 **Critical Thinking and Decision Making**
Imagine you were the professor. Make a list of reasons why you would or wouldn't admit Kim. Compare the pros and cons and reach a decision on whether to admit Kim. Justify your decision.

GRAMMAR

PASSIVES REVIEW

1 Match the sentences 1–6 with the reasons a–f for using the passive or active.

1 I worked hard at school.
2 The new education law has been approved by the government.
3 He'll be arriving late to the exam.
4 This exam seems harder than last year!
5 The winning poster will be chosen by the art undergraduates.
6 The library is being painted.

We use the passive when …

a we don't need to say who carries out an action
b we want to highlight who carries out an action
c we don't want the agent to be the main focus on the sentence

But we use an active form with …

d the future progressive
e verbs with no objects
f state verbs

2 Change the sentences from active to passive voice when possible. Only include *by* when the agent is important.

1 My school is in a multicultural neighbourhood.
2 Students speak many languages in my school.
3 The students are organising a special event to celebrate multilingualism.
4 This event will take place on the 27th March, International Day of Multilingualism.
5 Over 100 families attended the event last year.
6 Students have prepared posters, songs and talks in their home languages for the event.
7 They are going to hold a party on Saturday afternoon.
8 They'll send the invitations by email today.

CAUSATIVES

3 Tick the sentences which use the causative.

1 The school got the classroom decorated before the start of term.
2 The education department had the curriculum revised to include more projects.
3 More field trips have to be included in undergraduate degrees.
4 The school had their computers updated.
5 The parent got their child tutored in maths.

4 Read the anecdote about exams. Underline eight examples of the causative.

Lucy was determined to pass her physics finals, but she knew she couldn't do it alone. She had the key points emailed to her by her teacher so she could have her tutor review all the difficult topics with her, making sure she understood every concept. To help even more, she also had the most challenging physics equations explained to her by her brother, who was much better than her! It was then she realised she was going to have to get her calculator fixed; it really made things quicker.

To stay organised, she had her mother create a study schedule for her, ensuring she did some practice every day. The day before the exam, she even got her teacher to give her extra practice tests to build her confidence.

On the day of the exam, Lucy was nervous, but when the results finally came in, she was thrilled to see she had passed. She went straight to her laptop and had four nice thank you cards personalised, one for her teacher, tutor, brother and mum. It was clear that getting others involved had helped her succeed.

5 **>>> STRETCH!** Correct the underlined errors 1–8 in the text.

Not everyone needs to go to university to achieve success. Think about the last time you ¹ <u>fixed your cooker</u>, went to the bakery or had your hair styled. It's vocational training that ² <u>required</u> for those jobs, not an undergraduate degree. In fact, many industries have specialised training programmes which ³ <u>were been designed</u> to equip individuals with the necessary job skills without requiring a graduate education. An advantage of this is that hands-on experience ⁴ <u>can gained</u> much earlier, allowing young people to enter the workforce sooner. Additionally, the costs of higher education ⁵ <u>can be mean</u> many students won't ⁶ <u>have their student loans paid off</u> until they are in their thirties. This is another reason why it may not be a bad idea to ⁷ <u>get these options explaining</u> to you by a school career advisor before you apply to university.

In today's diverse economy, experience and practical knowledge are highly valued. Therefore, the assumption that university must be attended by everyone with the grades ⁸ <u>has being increasingly challenged.</u>

READING AND USE OF ENGLISH

EXAM TASK — READING AND USE OF ENGLISH PART 4

1 For questions 1–6, complete the second sentence so that it has a similar meaning to the first sentence, using the word given. Do not change the word given. You must use between three and six words, including the word given. There is an example (0).

0 Maria did a degree in geography even though she didn't have much interest in it.
SPITE
Maria did a degree in geography _in spite of her lack_ of interest in it.

1 After the long summer vacation, the students found it strange to have to study again.
USED
After the long summer vacation, it took the students a while to _____ again.

2 I regret the fact that I couldn't go on the last field trip to an archaeological site.
ABLE
I wish _____ go on the last field trip to an archaeological site.

3 It'd be a good idea to have an eye test if you can't read the board from the back of the classroom.
TESTED
You ought _____ if you can't read the board from the back of the classroom.

4 The deadlines aren't very flexible so students can't spend long on assignments.
ONLY
If _____ flexible, students could spend longer on assignments.

5 I made a mistake not studying psychology as my university degree.
MAJORED
I _____ university.

6 The teachers suspected Joe of getting someone else to write his essays.
BEEN
The teachers suspected that Joe's essays _____ him, but someone else.

VOCABULARY

EDUCATION – VERBS AND VERB PHRASES

1 Complete the conversation with the correct form of the words and phrases in the box.

> acquire knowledge   assess   carry out research
> cram   drop out   know your subject inside out
> memorise   secure a place   show initiative
> submit

A: Have you read this article? It's about the ways colleges might change in the future.

B: Does it mention being ¹_____ on groupwork? That would be a good idea. Being a good communicator and ²_____ should count towards grades, for sure.

B: Not exactly that, no …

A: Is it about using AI so we don't have to ³_____ so many dates and equations, then? I've read articles like that before. In fact, writing about that on my application helped me ⁴_____ on this course. I had to show I was interested in future technologies.

A: No. This journalist ⁵_____ a study into new workplace practices and how they could be applied to education. One idea is the four-day week. It's said that teenagers need more rest to ⁶_____, something that has also been proved to make big companies more productive. Cool, huh?

B: It is! I wish we had that. It might mean fewer students would ⁷_____ too. Some people get so tired at the end of term at college. And on top of that, that's when we have to ⁸_____ lots of assignments.

A: Right? The other idea is to shorten college holidays. They say it will mean less ⁹_____ for exams, more time to revise at a decent pace. It might mean people really get to ¹⁰_____, instead of just learning something for a day and forgetting it.

B: Shorter holidays? No, thanks! But the other ideas are cool!

UNIT 4 YOU LIVE, YOU LEARN | 35

LISTENING

1 Match the photos to the words in the box.

> coastline   cottage   fossil   mountain range   soil   quarry   safety goggles

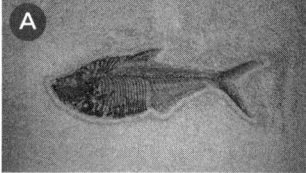

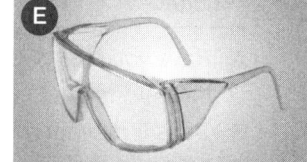

EXAM TIP

Part 2 answers are either a word or a short phrase of no more than three words. If you write four words in the gap, think how the answer can be shortened.

✓ EXAM TASK   LISTENING PART 2

2 🔊 4.1 You will hear a geology student called Suki Myers talking about a field trip she went on as part of her course. For questions 1–8, complete the sentences with a word or short phrase.

GEOLOGY FIELD TRIP TO SOMERSET

- Suki's earlier interest in ancient ¹_____ meant she was particularly happy to go to Somerset for the field trip.

- On the first day, Suki took great pride in identifying ²_____ very successfully.

- Suki says the students all gained a lot from using different types of equipment such as ³_____ to learn more about the rocks.

- Among the sketching methods they practised, Suki says that making ⁴_____ sketches of rock was particularly difficult.

- The students had to give their ⁵_____ in to their tutors after finishing the fieldwork each day.

- Suki felt stunned by the number of fossil remains of ⁶_____ in the quarry they explored.

- Because the stone of buildings in the area was ⁷_____ in colour, Suki says this made them very distinctive.

- Suki uses the term ⁸_____ to describe what she learnt most from the field trip.

3 What would you enjoy most about a field trip like this? Use words from Exercise 1 in your answer.

WRITING
A PROPOSAL

1 Answer the questions below.
1. What career would you like to pursue?
2. Do you know what your friends want to do when they are older?
3. What do you need to consider when you are choosing your future career?

2 Complete the sentences about proposals.
1. The person who will normally read a proposal is a *friend / person of authority*.
2. Proposals usually *have / don't have* headings to help the reader follow them.
3. Proposals should be written in a *neutral-formal / informal* style.
4. The aim of a proposal is to say what you *saw happen / want to happen*.
5. A proposal tries to *explain a situation to the reader / persuade the reader* to take action.

3 Underline the persuasive language in the extracts from a proposal.
1. Choosing a university course requires careful thought to avoid deeply regretting it later. The enormous pressure of this choice can leave some people feeling distressed.
2. Unfortunately, there is widespread belief that success is only found by going to university. This means that other options, such as vocational training, are not nearly explored enough.

EXAM TIP
Including passive forms in your writing will make it sound more formal.

4 Rewrite the proposal extracts using the passive.
1. This proposal will suggest how we can solve this problem.
2. Students' friends may pressure them into choosing similar subjects.
3. There are many reasons why career talks could help students.
4. This would prepare students for job opportunities.
5. If you gave students this opportunity, many would take it.

5 Read the exam task below and plan your proposal. Make notes for each paragraph. Remember to include paragraph headings.

1 Introduction	
2 Explain the problems	
3 Suggest solutions	
4 Conclusion	

EXAM TASK — WRITING PART 2

Many students at your college have difficulty deciding what career to go into after leaving school. The school director has asked you to write a proposal outlining the kinds of problems students have with this and suggesting how the school could guide students in making their career choices.

6 Write your proposal. Write your answer in 220–260 words.

SELF-EVALUATION

Check your writing:

Content: Have you covered all the points asked for? Have you written about at least two problems and how to overcome them? ☹ ☹ 😐 ☺

Communication: Can the reader clearly see your opinion? Is the style appropriate for a proposal? ☹ ☹ 😐 ☺

Organisation: Is the text well-organised and linked? Have you included headings? Are the final recommendations linked to the previous paragraphs? ☹ ☹ 😐 ☺

Language: Have you used a variety of structures and vocabulary? Have you included some new language from this unit? ☹ ☹ 😐 ☺

BUT THE GOOD NEWS IS ...

1 GETTING STARTED

My partner is: _____

Do you and your partner agree with Confucius's statement? Why? / Why not?

2 THINK

But the good news is ...

I'm working with: _____

Our group:
Reasons some people don't have access to education:
_____
_____
_____

Were any of these mentioned in the text about Anee?

It's important to generate hope because ...
_____
_____

How did the text about Anee make you feel?

3 EXPLORE

What?
_____
_____
_____

Where?
_____
_____

Who?
_____
_____

Positive initiatives around the world

How did it generate hope?
_____
_____
_____

Our group chose this as the best example of generating hope!

TIP Start by talking as a group about group about positive initiatives you have heard of. Think about local or international stories you've read/seem in the news. You can also search online for more information.

38 | **UNIT 4** YOU LIVE, YOU LEARN

4 DEVELOP

EXPLORING SUSTAINABILITY 2

Plan your poster

Notes from our group discussion:
_____
_____
_____

> Have you looked back at the Oracy task in Unit 3 to help with your group discussion?

Image ideas for the poster:
_____
_____

What we can include on the poster:
_____
_____
_____
_____

My role in making the poster:
_____

TIP — **Professional development and management**
Manage your time when you make a poster by setting time limits for the group, and planning a mid-task meeting to check how everyone is doing.

> How will you divide the work of making the poster? Will it be on paper or designed online?

5 PRESENT

After the presentation:

Things we did well:
_____
_____

Things we could improve on:
_____
_____
_____

> Does everyone know what they're doing?
> Do we know which order we're presenting in?
> Have we got everything we need?

I looked at all the other posters and I especially liked _____ because _____.

SELF-EVALUATION

I can ...
- identify and explain a local or global initiative which generate hope. ○
- identify, gather and organise relevant information. ○
- work constructively in a group poster task to generate hope in myself and others. ○

UNIT 4 YOU LIVE, YOU LEARN

UNIT 5 BEING ME

VOCABULARY

PERSONALITY

1 Complete the conversation with the correct words from the box.

> an introvert / introverted   an extrovert / extroverted   conscientious   frugal   idealistic   impulsive   insecure   methodical   obstinate   placid   resolute   tolerant

A: So, what do you think about this next candidate for class president, Aimar?

B: Well, he's very ¹_____. I mean, his assignments are always top quality and on time, and he's ²_____ with writing and editing. He'd be great at writing proposals.

A: True. He used to be more ³_____ about his abilities and get shy in group discussions, but now he's quite ⁴_____ about getting his opinions across. He keeps going until he makes his point. But he's also ⁵_____ of what others say too; he isn't rude or anything.

B: And is he experienced at handling money? The class president plans the end of school party so being ⁶_____ with funds is super important.

A: Let's ask him in the interview.

2 Complete the sentences with an adjective from Exercise 1 and a preposition.

1 Nyra was very _____ _____ different opinions in class discussions.
2 Ben was _____ _____ all his spending, so he saved loads.
3 He remained _____ _____ his decision to leave; he was certain about it.
4 Sometimes I'm too _____ _____ friendship. I want everyone to behave perfectly all the time.
5 My teacher is _____ _____ her marking. She's very organised.
6 Don't be _____ _____ making mistakes, they help you learn.

3 Write a short text describing a friend or family member's personality. Use the adjectives from Exercise 1.

4 **Emotional Intelligence** Is there anything you'd like to change about your personality? How could you do this? Make a plan.

READING

1 Read the text on page 42 quickly and put the topics a–e in the order they are mentioned.

a anxiety and depression _____
b the big five test _____
c talking to strangers _____
d twins _____
e smartphones _____

EXAM TASK — READING AND USE OF ENGLISH PART 7

EXAM TIP

The link between the missing paragraph and the text is not always grammatical – it can also be lexical or logical.

2 You are going to read an extract from an article about research into people's personalities. Six paragraphs have been removed from the extract. Choose from the paragraphs A–G the one which fits each gap (1–6). There is one extra paragraph which you do not need to use.

RESEARCH SUGGESTS THAT YOUR PERSONALITY IS NOT SET IN STONE

Have you ever wished you could be better organised or more sociable? Perhaps you're a constant worrier, and you'd prefer to be a little more carefree? If any of these thoughts ring true, you're far from alone. Research suggests that many people would like to change some element of their personality.

1

Recent research, however, challenges this expectation of personality's permanence. With certain methods, and enough effort, people can change. The research centres on what is known as the theory of the 'big five'. These are five fundamental traits: extroversion – how outgoing and sociable you are; conscientiousness – how organised and disciplined you are; agreeableness – how concerned you are with social harmony; neuroticism – how nervous and sensitive you are; and openness to experience – how imaginative and curious you are. These are assessed via a test that measures where people score on a continuum from low to high for each trait.

2

Our genes almost certainly play a role in determining all this, which is why people's personalities often reflect their biological parents' traits, and why identical twins are more similar than non-identical siblings. The social environment also plays a part, but its influence was once thought to end in early adulthood, as the brain reached maturity.

3

In a series of groundbreaking studies, they showed that, with certain interventions, such as regularly repeating activities that reflect the personality traits people wish to adopt, characteristics can be modified and developed. An introvert who wished to be more extroverted, for example, might have to introduce themselves to a stranger once a week. Someone wishing to be more conscientious might write a to-do list or proofread their emails before sending them on a daily basis.

4

In one trial of nearly 400 people, participants accepted an average of two challenges each week. Provided they actually completed them, the traits they desired to change shifted in the right direction, according to a standard questionnaire. Similarly, exciting results were seen in a later study, which used smartphones to coach participants in modifying their desired traits. Researchers found that nine months later, the subjects showed significant developments, which continued after the experiments formally ended.

5

Another reason for optimism relates to mental health. In conditions such as depression and anxiety people often have negative feelings they feel cannot be changed. US researchers selected around 100 participants who experienced anxiety or depression. These people took a brief course that explained the science of how brains can change, read statements from people who described ways their negative feelings had changed for the better, and completed worksheets to consolidate what they had learned.

6

However, it does suggest that it is a useful tool for building greater psychological resilience. Knowing methods like these can work is reassuring and indicates that personality is to some extent within our own hands. Our genes and upbringing may predispose us to certain traits, but we also have the capacity to shape our future selves.

A However, if this idea were true, you would not expect adults' personalities to change naturally over time, and it wouldn't be possible to mould personality at will. Yet, that is exactly what some psychology researchers have found.

B These effects strongly suggest that we become what we do again and again. News of this unexpected but proven ability to change how our minds work should be cause for optimism for anyone who wishes they were a bit more sociable, organised, or happy-go-lucky.

C Instead, this may be crucial to enable people to change. And if such thoughts and behaviour are repeated often enough, it becomes increasingly likely that the new ways of thinking and behaving will extend into other aspects of life.

D Educating them in this way about the potential for improving their emotional states sent them in a more positive direction, with encouraging outcomes that were repeated in other settings. It should be said that teaching people about personality growth is not a miracle cure.

E In the past, such desires appeared to be futile. Our character was thought to be formed in childhood and to remain fixed throughout our lives. Like the proverb that says a leopard cannot change its spots, our virtues and flaws were believed to be set in stone.

F The fact that people's scores on these specific characteristics can predict important outcomes in life has been shown in many studies based on this particular psychological model. For example, high scores in one might predict how well people do at school. A score indicating a predisposition for stress could predict effects on health. Likewise, being easy to get along with is a good predictor of doing well at work.

G While tasks like this may sound insignificant, the aim is for the thinking patterns and behaviours they generate to become habitual. And the evidence so far suggests that they work remarkably well.

GRAMMAR

GERUNDS AND INFINITIVES

1 Complete the sentences using the correct form of the verb in brackets.

1 She reminded him not _____ (be) late.
2 I don't mind us _____ (be) frugal sometimes.
3 I can't imagine you _____ (act) so stubbornly.
4 People expect introverts _____ (like) reading, but it isn't always true.
5 The book taught me _____ (feel) grateful for the simple joys of life.
6 I'd appreciate you _____ (be) more tolerant, please!
7 They want us _____ (say) when we're annoyed.
8 Do that again, and you'll risk friends _____ (leave) the party.
9 I dislike people _____ (tell) me how to act.

2 Some verbs change their meaning if they are followed by the gerund or infinitive with *to*. Complete the rules with the verbs in the box.

go on   mean   remember   stop   try

1 _____ + gerund is used to talk about when you don't do something anymore.
   _____ + infinitive with *to* is used to talk about interrupting one thing to do something else.
2 _____ + gerund is used to talk about what is necessary.
   _____ + infinitive with *to* is used to talk about intentions.
3 _____ + gerund is used in the same way as *continue to*.
   _____ + infinitive with *to* is used to talk about what someone will do later.
4 _____ + gerund is used when you're doing something as an experiment.
   _____ + infinitive with *to* is used to say something is difficult but you're making an effort.
5 _____ + gerund is used when you have a memory of something.
   _____ + infinitive with *to* is used to say there is something you need to do.

3 Choose the correct options to complete the sentences.

1 If only I could stop *to be* / *being* lazy!
2 I stopped *to help* / *helping* the woman with her bags. She thanked me.
3 I didn't mean *to appear* / *appearing* so obstinate, we could have watched the film you wanted!
4 Being an introvert doesn't mean *not to have* / *not having* confidence.
5 He's so obstinate, he'll go on *to be* / *being* a politician!
6 I'm going to go on *to be* / *being* myself, I won't change my personality for anyone!
7 Try *to rehearse* / *rehearsing* in front of the mirror, it'll give you confidence.
8 You should try *to be* / *being* less idealistic in life.
9 Remember *to save* / *saving* your answers before you exit the test.
10 Do you remember *to be* / *being* impulsive when we were young?

PARTICIPLE CLAUSES

4 Replace the relative clause in the sentences with a present or past participle clause.

1 The person who chooses the team leader needs to think about their personality.
2 This poster, which is presented by Axel, is about extroverts and introverts.
3 The documentary, which showed tests done by identical twins, was really interesting.
4 Everyone who will take the personality test today should stand in this queue.
5 The film was about twins who met each other for the first time.
6 The explanation that the teacher gave helped me to understand introversion.

5 Rewrite the sentences using present or past participle clauses.

1 She felt tired, so she took a nap.
2 Mika knew her friend loved reading, and so she bought him a book.
3 Since they did not want to be late, they left the house an hour early.
4 Boma's friends encouraged her to sign up for the talent competition, and she did.
5 She heard her name and turned around to see her friend waving.
6 He thanked the crowd. He was filled with happiness.
7 She fell asleep on the sofa because she was exhausted from the day of exams.
8 The company were impressed by the candidate and offered him the job.

6 Rewrite the sentences using perfect participle clauses.

1 Jason grew up in a big family, so he was always happy to share.
2 She felt nervous the week before school started. She had just moved schools.
3 He called his mum because he realised he'd be late.
4 He knew how to calm horses as he'd had lots of experience working with them.
5 She had been too idealistic in the past, but now she was very different.
6 She felt emotionally tired. She'd met so many new people.

7 >>> STRETCH! Choose the correct options to complete the text.

How is personality connected to music tastes?

Firstly, studies have shown that certain personality traits are strongly correlated with specific music genres. For example, research by psychologists found that people who try ¹ *to have / having* new experiences often tend ² *to prefer / preferring* more complex music genres, such as classical or jazz music. In contrast, those who are extremely extroverted are more likely to enjoy energetic and rhythmic music, such as pop and hip-hop.

³ *Relating / Related* lyrics to personality, a study from the University of Cambridge found that people who prefer songs with rebellious or aggressive lyrics often score higher in traits like openness and agreeableness. This suggests that people may use music to express or explore parts of their personality not normally ⁴ *shown / is shown*.

Also, some research says that the music people listen to during their teenage years can impact personality development. Adolescents ⁵ *listened / listening* to music with positive, empowering messages may develop higher self-esteem and more optimistic world views. The message? Go on ⁶ *enjoying / to enjoy* positive music!

These studies suggest that the relationship between music and personality is complex, ⁷ *having served / serving* as a mirror, as a way to explore, and by shaping our identities.

💬 5   ♡ 20   🔁 9

VOCABULARY

NEGATIVE PREFIXES

1 Complete the sentences with a negative prefix from the box.

de- dis- il- im- in- ir-
mis- over- un- under-

1 _____respect has no place in true friendship.
2 In most countries, it's _____legal to bully others on social media.
3 Arguments with friends can cause _____ease, but real friends work through it.
4 A long lasting friendship without any problems at all is an _____possibility.
5 True friendship is often _____rated, but it's the support we need in tough times.
6 The _____use of social media during school hours led to stricter rules about bringing mobile phones.
7 Sometimes the _____ability to communicate openly can hurt a friendship.
8 If social media causes you stress, it's a good idea to _____activate the comments.
9 Never _____estimate the power of a hug.
10 I found a lot of research papers about personality, but they were all _____relevant to my essay topic.

2 Complete the text with words from Exercise 1.

You might not realise it, but emotions affect our physical as well as mental health, a fact that is often ¹_____. For instance, depression can slow down the body's natural healing processes. When someone suggests that your stress about assignments is why you keep getting a cold, you might dismiss this comment as silly and ²_____. However, when we experience sadness, ³_____ or anger our body responds physically by releasing stress hormones that elevate blood pressure. Perhaps that's where the term 'heartache' comes from. Luckily, stress management techniques can help ⁴_____ the body's response of releasing these hormones. The ⁵_____ to manage these emotions is the issue, so if we work on dealing with them, we can lessen the impact on our bodies. In short, it's a complete ⁶_____ to separate emotions and the body – they're connected. Next time you start feeling negative because someone ⁷_____ you, or argues with you or you have a deadline coming, feel and manage your emotions. You'll feel healthier!

LISTENING

1 You are going to hear an interview with an actor about how his personality changes when he's acting. If you were the presenter, what would you ask? Write four questions.

2 Match the words and phrases in the box to the definitions.

> authority figure   cameras stop rolling
> dive in   frown   have people lining up
> linger   shooting   upbringing

1 a facial gesture showing sadness or worry, using your eyebrows
2 take a long time to leave or disappear
3 have many people interested in something
4 a person in a position of power, e.g. a police officer, judge or teacher
5 to start talking about or do something immediately
6 the way someone is treated or taught as a child
7 to stop recording a film
8 the period in which a film is being made

3 🔊 5.1 Listen to the podcast and take notes. Are any of your questions mentioned?

4 Match the sentences halves to make strategies for note-taking tasks. Tick any you used in Exercise 3. Choose another strategy to use for Exercise 5.

1 I write nouns and verbs to
2 When I listen for the first time, I write
3 I use bullet points so I don't have to
4 I use symbols, lines and

a write full sentences.
b down the questions.
c abbreviations to connect ideas.
d understand key points.

5 🔊 5.1 Listen again. Add to your notes.

6 Read sentences 1–5. Use your notes to decide if they are true or false.

1 Adam says that the hard work starts when he gets to the movie set.
2 Adam sometimes uses fake tears.
3 Adam thinks that looking into a character's past is important.
4 Adam says that characters can affect him even after a film is made.
5 Adam has studied how different languages affect a person's character.

7 Use your notes to finish the summary sentences.

1 Roles in which Adam plays someone not like him …
2 It can be exhausting …
3 Creating a personality profile of a character means …
4 Relaxing after filming is important because if not …
5 Having learnt Spanish from a family member, Adam agrees …

8 💼 **Communication** When you interview someone, it's important to make an effort to understand the person you are talking to. Do you think the presenter did a good job at creating a connection in the interview? What things did she do well? What things would you do differently?

WRITING

AN INFORMAL EMAIL

1 Look at the phrases in the box. Are they used towards the start or end of informal emails? How do you say the phrases in your language?

How are you doing?	It's great to hear from you.
That's all for now	
Long time no see!	That's nearly it for me.
Chat online soon?	Got to go, but …
It's been ages since I …	

2 How do you say the phrases in Exercise 1 in your language?

EXAM TIP

Don't translate opening and closing phrases from your language. They might be expressed differently in English!

3 Read the exam task. How do the people know each other? Which do you think is the more appropriate register: formal or informal?

4 Choose the more informal option to complete the sentences.

1 *Without a doubt / Of course,* I've changed a lot!
2 *I'd also say / Furthermore, I would argue* that I'm more extroverted.
3 *I reckon I'm pretty / I'm said to be rather* similar to my dad.
4 *How about in / Would you mind telling me about* your family?
5 *I hope to hear from you soon / Let's chat soon,* I hope!

5 Read the exam task again and plan your email. Make notes for each paragraph.

1	Opening	
2	Answer one question	
3	Answer another question	
4	Answer another question	
5	Closing section	

✓ EXAM TASK WRITING PART 2

You have received an email from an old friend who was in your class at primary school.

… I'm sure you've changed a lot since we were little. I'm studying psychology now and I'm doing a university project on people's personalities. I'd love to know what you're like now. How would you describe yourself? Are you more introverted or extroverted Who do you take after in your family? …

6 Write your email in reply. Write your answer in 220–260 words.

SELF-EVALUATION

Check your writing:

Content: Have you answered all three questions asked? Have you referenced the time when you knew each other? Have you asked questions?

Communication: Are your answers clear to the reader? Have you followed the conventions of an informal email?

Organisation: Is the text well-organised and linked? Is there a good flow of ideas? ☹ ☺ ☺ ☺

Language: Have you used a variety of structures and vocabulary? Is your language informal? Have you included some new language from this unit?

A MODERATED DISCUSSION

1 SETTING UP

I'm working with:
_____
_____

My role is:
_____

In my role I want to mention ... /
As moderator I plan to ask:
_____
_____
_____
_____
_____

2 AGREE ON GROUND RULES

Collaboration and Teamwork

What should the ground rules for this discussion be?

TIP Think about what the other people could say in response to your statements. Plan counter arguments.

3 ACTIVE LISTENING

How can you use body language to show you are listening?
_____
_____
_____

How else can you show you are listening?
_____
_____

What short phrases can you use to show you are listening?
_____
_____
_____

ORACY 3

4 ASKING A RANGE OF QUESTIONS

What open questions could you ask the others?
_____
_____
_____

It's good to ask open questions because …
_____
_____

It's good to ask follow-up questions because …
_____
_____

What question can you use to clarify?
_____
_____
_____

After the discussion:
I talked to my classmate _____ about what he/she contributed, and she/he gave me feedback. I need to think more about …
_____
_____
_____

What question can you use to dig deeper?
_____
_____
_____

5 FEEDBACK

I've decided with my classmate _____ that we'll give each other feedback.

After the discussion:

3 interesting things that were mentioned:
_____
_____
_____

2 adjectives to describe how I feel now:
I feel …
_____
_____

1 point I made really well:
_____

SELF-EVALUATION

I can …
- follow the agreed ground rules in a moderated discussion. ○
- play my role well. ○
- use active listening strategies. ○
- ask a range of questions. ○

UNIT 5 BEING ME | 47

UNIT 6 LET'S CELEBRATE!

VOCABULARY
CELEBRATIONS

1 Match the words from Unit 6 to the photos.

1 festivities
2 feast
3 transition
4 milestone
5 spectacle
6 ritual

A

B

C

D

E

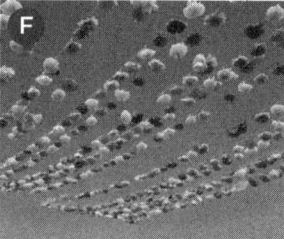
F

2 Complete the phrases from Unit 6 with the correct verb. The first letter is given to help you.

1 b_____ with tradition
2 c_____ of age
3 f_____ on/in a day/month
4 h_____ a party
5 m_____ an occasion
6 u_____ a tradition

3 Complete the text with words and phrases from Exercises 1 and 2.

All through his childhood, Emile's birthday, which ¹_____ on December 25th, would often get lost in the spectacle of the holiday season. While his friends ²_____ big _____ with dancing and games, Emile's special day was blended with Christmas ³_____, such as all the family spending a night together decorating the tree, and although they exchanged presents, he only got one, never two. The Christmas ⁴_____ and cake was just that, for Christmas, nothing to do with his birthday.

As he approached his 18th, which is a ⁵_____ birthday in France, he got an acceptance letter from university and started looking at student flats. This year would be a significant ⁶_____ in his life. Emile decided it was time to ⁷_____ and do something completely different. It was a 'big' birthday, and most people would remember this ⁸_____ event, like the first day of school, or a wedding, or a graduation, with a party. If you don't ⁹_____ like turning 18, will you regret it later? He decided that he would, and so he chose to celebrate it in February! Finally, he fully enjoyed his day without competing with Christmas.

4 >>> STRETCH! Answer the questions. Use full sentences, and explain when needed.

1 In your country, what birthdays are considered 'coming of age' birthdays?
2 What three things have been milestones in your life so far?
3 What day of the week does your birthday fall on this year?
4 If someone says, 'Let's have a feast at the weekend!' what would you want to eat?
5 What are the next festivities coming up in your country?
6 When was the last time you hosted a party? What was it for?

READING

1 Read the text. Match the headings 1–5 to the paragraphs A–E.

1 event
2 planning
3 evaluation
4 preparation
5 permissions

2 Read the text again. Which paragraph (A–E) mentions:

1 visits by the local council to festivals
2 a presentation to the local authorities
3 the types of people who make up a committee
4 giving money to charity
5 the fact that environmentally friendly festivals are favoured
6 asking visitors for their opinion
7 advertising for a festival

3 Use the words in bold in the text to complete the definitions.

1 A _____ is an official document allowing you to do something.
2 A _____ is someone who sells something, often outdoors.
3 A _____ is a plan for how much money you have, and how you will spend it.
4 _____ is collecting money for a purpose, usually for charity.
5 The _____ of a venue/area is the maximum amount of people that it can hold.

Community festivals — INFORMATION SHEET

Information to date as of March

Organizing a community festival in this region is a multi-step process. The process can be divided into several key stages. Please use this document to help plan your festival.

A _____ This must begin several months before the festival. We recommend that a committee is formed, composed of community leaders and volunteers. This committee is responsible for setting the date and theme of the festival. The committee next creates a **budget** that considers costs for decorations, entertainment, food **vendors**, and other necessary services. Fundraising efforts, such as local business sponsorships, are also discussed at this stage.

B _____ This important stage involves two chosen members of your festival committee meeting with our events team. During this meeting you will present your full proposal for the event to secure a **permit** from the local council department for your festival. The decision whether to grant a permit depends on many factors including **capacity**, the date it falls on, refreshments and type of festivities, and if it meets sustainability targets.

C _____ Once permits are granted, specific tasks are given to each committee member. It's advisable to meet regularly to discuss these, as there are many overlaps. For instance, the person booking musicians will also need to talk with the committee member responsible for organising electricity and safety measures. The committee should also divide efforts in promoting the festival through various channels, including social media, local newspapers, and posters around the community.

D _____ This is the day of the festival. The committee and volunteers arrive early to set up stages, entrance areas, and traffic blocks if required. Decorations are hung, and vendors set up their stalls. As the festival begins, the committee members must be responsible for making sure that everything runs smoothly. A council event representative will do checks throughout the day.

E _____ Reviewing the success of the festival is crucial to an event. The committee should discuss what went well and what could be improved for future events. Financial records are reviewed to ensure that all expenses were covered and to assess the effectiveness of the **fundraising** efforts. Feedback from attendees and vendors is also collected, providing valuable insights for the next festival. Any leftover funds are typically saved for future events or donated to a community cause.

By following these steps, our local communities can successfully bring people together to uphold traditions, mark special occasions and celebrate together.

✉ Please contact the events department with any questions: events@yourlocalcouncil.com

UNIT 6 LET'S CELEBRATE! | 49

GRAMMAR

CONDITIONALS REVIEW

1 Match the question halves. What kind of conditionals are they?

1. If the event attracts more visitors,
2. If it had rained during the performance,
3. If it rains during an event,
4. If we were more organised,
5. If you'd saved more money,
6. If you could go to any festival in the world,

a what happens?
b which one would you go to?
c will they expand it next year?
d what would we have done?
e would we have won that talent competition?
f would you want to come with me?

2 Rewrite the underlined parts of the anecdote using an appropriate conditional.

It was supposed to be the garden party of the year, but things started to go wrong quickly. ¹Sara didn't check the weather forecast, so she didn't realise a storm was coming. As the guests arrived, the skies darkened. Sara thought to herself, ²'Rain will make everyone go home. What should I do?'
Looking back, ³renting a big tent would have been a good idea, for people to stand under. But she hadn't, so when the rain came, everyone crammed into her small living room. Things were going OK until suddenly darkness hit. Someone joked, ⁴'Maybe staying at home was a good idea. I didn't know it would be like this!'
Then a friend had an idea. Using earphones and an app to connect, they all joined him in listening to the same music. It was a silent disco! After they'd danced for hours, people went home. As Sara cleaned up, she thought, ⁵'Hosting a party like this again ... Would I? Yes, probably!'

INVERTED CONDITIONALS

3 Match the sentence halves about being on a festival committee. Then decide if the sentences refer to the past, present or future.

1. Were there more volunteers,
2. Had you booked more vendors,
3. Should the city council come,
4. Had I known this would be so much work,
5. Should ticket prices drop,

a we'll show them the permits.
b I wouldn't have volunteered!
c more people would come.
d the stage would get set up quicker.
e we'd have enough food.

4 Complete each sentence with *Should*, *Were* or *Had*.

1. _____ the weather be good, we'll have the end of term party outdoors.
2. _____ we to raise enough money, we could hire a band to play.
3. _____ last year's party committee not used the theme of superheroes, I would love to do that this year.
4. _____ we to go for a theme of nature, would everyone be happy with that?
5. _____ I to make the poster, would that be OK with you?
6. _____ we not decide everything today, could we meet again tomorrow?

5 Complete the text with the correct phrases from the box.

> Had you seen   Should the participants be lucky
> the race would be   they might cross
> Were the hill to be   Were you to go
> you might see   you'd remember it

¹_____ to Gloucestershire, England, in May, ²_____ the strange tradition which is upheld there: the Cooper's Hill Cheese-Rolling Festival. This crazy spectacle involves rolling a large wheel of cheese down a steep hill while participants race to catch it. ³_____ a video of a previous event, ⁴_____! The cheese, which is rolled from the top of Cooper's Hill, reaches speeds of up to 70 miles per hour, and many people fall down the hill. Unable to catch it. ⁵_____ enough to avoid injury, ⁶_____ the finish line first and claim the cheese as their prize. The steep hill is the festival's unique appeal. ⁷_____ less steep, ⁸_____ far less dramatic, and the cheese wouldn't achieve such impressive speeds.

READING AND USE OF ENGLISH

EXAM TASK — READING AND USE OF ENGLISH PART 4

1 For questions 1–6, complete the second sentence so that it has a similar meaning to the first sentence, using the word given. Do not change the word given. You must use between three and six words, including the word given. Here is an example (0).

0 I really don't mind whether we celebrate New Year or not. **DIFFERENCE**
It really _makes no difference to_ me whether we celebrate New Year or not.

1 The fireworks display had to be cancelled due to the heavy rain. **HAVE**
The fireworks display _____ be cancelled if it hadn't rained so much.

2 A professional dressmaker is making my wedding dress as I want it to be really beautiful. **MADE**
I want a really beautiful wedding dress, so _____ by a professional dressmaker.

3 If the ceremony doesn't follow tradition, some guests will be disappointed. **BREAK**
Should there _____ at the ceremony, some guests will be disappointed.

4 You definitely would have regretted not accepting the invitation to the prize-giving ceremony. **TURNED**
Had _____ the invitation to the prize-giving ceremony, you definitely would have regretted it.

5 To have enough money for a gift for your parents' wedding anniversary, you'd better start saving up. **ABLE**
If you don't save up, _____ to get a gift for your parents' wedding anniversary.

6 As long as it doesn't last too long, most people enjoy listening to a speech. **ON**
If a speech _____ ages, people tend not to enjoy it so much.

VOCABULARY
DESCRIBING CELEBRATIONS

1 Cross out the noun that does not collocate with the adjective.

1 an atmospheric mood / setting / person / lighting
2 a customary song / gift / dance / tradition
3 an extravagant conversation / party / gift / person
4 a festive period / smile / season / meal
5 a flamboyant dancer / laugh / speaker / dress
6 a joyous smile / laugh / party / fail
7 (a) raucous party / singing / behaviour / request
8 a tranquil sea / storm / space / song
9 a vibrant poster / dance / calm / costume

2 Complete the text using words from Exercise 1.

Turning 18 is a significant milestone for anyone, and in many countries parents throw expensive, [1]_____ parties for their kids. In Scotland it is also [2]_____ for a boy to get his first kilt on his eighteenth. A kilt is a traditional Scottish piece of clothing, resembling a skirt. It is made from thick wool in [3]_____ colours, woven together in lines to create a pattern called 'tartan'. Kilts are worn at special occasions like important birthdays, weddings and graduations. Some say the somewhat [4]_____ outfit perfectly matches the [5]_____ singing and dancing of a Scottish party. Were you to picture someone wearing a kilt, you might imagine a piper next to a [6]_____ lake playing bagpipes, a traditional instrument. Far from being joyful, this instrument has a melancholy and [7]_____ sound.
Both the kilt and the bagpipes are symbols of a traditional Scotland.

UNIT 6 LET'S CELEBRATE!

LISTENING

1 🧳 **Professional Development and Management**
What skills does an event planner need to be successful at their job? Make a list.

2 Match the words and phrases from the interview to the definitions.

1 to wow someone
2 a blip
3 to dine
4 to know the ropes
5 hurdle
6 glitch
7 hiccup

a to know exactly what to do
b a big problem you need to overcome
c a little problem/a computer fault
d a little problem/a repeated noise when air is stuck and released from your throat
e to impress someone
f to have dinner (formal)
g a little problem

EXAM TIP

When the interviewer asks a new question, look at the next question in the task.

✅ EXAM TASK — LISTENING PART 3

3 🔊 6.1 You will hear an interview in which two event planners called Maya Mallik and Craig Damasio are talking about their work. For questions 1–6, choose the answer (A, B, C or D) which fits best according to what you hear.

1 Craig says that a key factor in organising a memorable event is to
   A provide the best food and drink possible.
   B arrange for some unexpected elements.
   C ensure the clients' ideas are included.
   D create an original central theme.

2 What does Maya say about organising her first celebrity wedding?
   A She was surprised mistakes went unnoticed.
   B She thinks she could have done better.
   C She was grateful to get plenty of help.
   D She thinks her success was due to luck.

3 When Maya organised a film director's party for his daughter, she felt
   A flattered by the comments in the press.
   B tempted to suggest an alternative venue.
   C concerned about the number of people invited.
   D confident the live performances would be popular.

4 When organising a film awards ceremony, Craig says that he was
   A enthusiastic about taking on a new challenge.
   B motivated by the attention it would receive.
   C worried about how to make it exceptional.
   D inspired by having a large budget.

5 What do Maya and Craig agree is the hardest part about attending events they organise?
   A relaxing and enjoying themselves
   B dealing with problems that arise
   C having to make last-minute changes
   D observing everything that's going on

6 When talking about corporate events, Craig and Maya both reveal their belief that
   A getting things perfect is a key aim.
   B imaginative approaches are effective.
   C experiencing technical issues is normal.
   D patience is essential at the planning stages.

WRITING

A REVIEW

1 Read the exam task. Which two topics could you write about, and why?

1. a bakery that sells creative wedding cakes
2. a restaurant you often order delivery food from
3. a nice restaurant you once had your birthday in
4. a restaurant your parents took you to after passing exams
5. a café that you and your friends love
6. a restaurant in Hawaii you'd love to go to

2 Read the model answer and underline the opinion phrases that the writer uses.

If you're looking for somewhere special to mark an occasion like a milestone birthday or wedding anniversary, I would definitely recommend Rock Street Lounge. I have visited it for several special occasions and it has always been a memorable experience. It's a very atmospheric restaurant, with a stylish feel and soft lighting, all of which make it perfect for a memorable night out, whether as a couple or a larger group.

The menu offers a wide range of international dishes, so there's something for everyone's taste. Not only are there freshly made sushi, curries, pizza and pasta, but they also have several dishes of the day on the menu, which are definitely worth trying.

The waiters and other staff are very friendly and attentive, making sure you have everything you need and they're always ready to offer suggestions if you're not sure what to choose to eat. One thing that could make the experience even better would be if they offered more dessert options. The current choices, such as tiramisu and chocolate mousse, are wonderful, but adding a few more would be a great way to improve the restaurant.

Overall, I wouldn't hesitate to recommend Rock Street Lounge for a special occasion. The inviting atmosphere, diverse menu, and great service make it a place that is well worth choosing.

EXAM TIP

To give your writing variety, use a range of phrases to introduce your opinions.

3 Read the task again and plan your review. Make notes for each paragraph.

1	Introduction	
2	Explain suitability for a special occasion	
3	Suggest an improvement(s) connected to special occasions	
4	Sum up and make a recommendation	

✓ EXAM TASK — WRITING PART 2

A website called Eating Out has asked for reviews of a restaurant that people would recommend for celebrating a special occasion. Write a review of a restaurant you know, describing the restaurant and explaining why you would recommend it for celebrating a special occasion. You should also suggest at least one way in which you think the restaurant could be improved.

4 Write your review in 220–260 words.

SELF-EVALUATION

Check your writing:

Content: Have you covered all the points asked for? What special occasion(s) have you recommended it for? Have you suggested improvements? ☹ 😐 🙂 😊

Communication: Is it clear why you think your choice of restaurant is right? Is the style appropriate for a review? ☹ 😐 🙂 😊

Organisation: Is the text well-organised and linked? Is there a good flow of ideas? ☹ 😐 🙂 😊

Language: Have you used a variety of structures and vocabulary? Have you included some new language from this unit? ☹ 😐 🙂 😊

GREEN FESTIVALS

1 GETTING STARTED

How can we make festivals more sustainable?

My partner is: _____

My partner and I think these events are ...
_____
_____
_____

TIP — **Communication**
After you've completed your mind map, explain it to someone <u>not</u> in your group. Talking about your work can help you organise your ideas and find the right words.

2 THINK

To organise a festival we need to consider ...

Leadership and global citizenship
Discuss – why are these things more sustainable?

3 EXPLORE

My group is ...

Location:
_____
Name:
_____
It's a festival of ...
_____
How is it more social and environmentally sustainable?
_____
_____
_____
_____

Sustainable festivals around the world

TIP Look into different ways each festival is sustainable, e.g. food/drink, power, waste reduction, advice for people, things for sale, community involvement, choice of activities, sponsorship, etc.

Location:
_____
Name:
_____
It's a festival of ...
_____
How is it more social and environmentally sustainable?
_____
_____
_____
_____

Have you found out about a variety of sustainable areas?

54 | UNIT 6 LET'S CELEBRATE!

4 DEVELOP

EXPLORING SUSTAINABILITY 3

Take turns to share your research.
Which are the best ideas?
Write them here:

_____
_____
_____
_____

Plan your infographic

Design ideas for the infographic:
_____
_____

What we can include:
_____
_____
_____

My role in making the infographic:
_____
_____

TIP Infographics make information easier to understand with charts, graphs and icons. With your group, discuss what data you will present, and how.

Have you looked back at the oracy task in Unit 3 to help in your group discussion?

How will you divide the work of making the infographic? Will it be on paper or designed online?

5 PRESENT

Does everyone know what they're doing?
Do we know which order we're presenting in?
Have we got everything we need?

Is our infographic easy to understand?
Is it engaging?
Does it contain all the information we want?

After the presentation

Things we did well:
_____
_____

Things we could improve:
_____
_____
_____

I looked at all the other posters and I especially liked … because …

SELF-EVALUATION

I can …
- identify, gather and organise relevant information about sustainable festivals. ○
- identify socially and environmentally sustainable alternatives. ○
- design and explain an imaginary festival with a strong focus on sustainability. ○
- work constructively in a group infographic task. ○

REVIEW 2 UNITS 4-6

GRAMMAR 1

1 Rewrite the questions in the passive when possible.

1 When was the last time your school organised a field trip for your class?
2 Has your school introduced any new rules this year?
3 Will you be doing any exams this week?
4 How do teachers grade your work, with percentages or comments?
5 Does your school have a good sports team?
6 What did you work hardest on this term?
7 Has anyone planned an end of term party?
8 When did the town build your school?

2 Complete the second sentence so that it has a similar meaning to the first sentence, using the word given. Do not change the word given. Use between three and five words, including the word given.

1 When applying to college, we advise asking someone else to review your application.
   REVIEWED
   When applying to college, we advise _____ by someone else.
2 We also recommend using an online spell checker.
   GETTING
   We also recommend _____ online.
3 To increase your chances of a place, tick the box that means the system will send your application to multiple colleges.
   HAVE
   To increase your chances of a place, tick the box to _____ to multiple colleges.
4 Once you get a place, ask the college finance department to explain your payment options.
   GET
   Once you get a place, _____ by the college finance department.
5 Finally, don't forget to request a room in a student residence!
   RESERVED
   Finally, don't forget to _____ for you in the student residence.

VOCABULARY 1

1 Choose the correct words to complete the dialogue.

Kam: So, tell the listeners of Uni Life podcast what the first week as an ¹*academic year / undergraduate* is like.

Dimitri: Well, the first week of the ²*academic year / syllabus* can be exciting but also overwhelming. As soon as I got the ³*syllabus / deadline* for my courses, I realised how much work was ahead.

Kam: ⁴*Assignments / Field trips* can be given in the first week, can't they?

Dimitri: Yes, and they were, with ⁵*finals / a deadline* for the week after. In your first year, there is nothing as big as ⁶*an assignment / a dissertation* to write, or ⁷*finals / scholarships* to study for, but you will have essays and exams. One thing that you really need to understand is the importance of avoiding ⁸*student loans / plagiarism* when writing. I'd learned the basics before, but now with AI tools it isn't always that clear what you can and can't use. That was interesting.

Kam: And I suppose managing money is something new too?

Dimitri: Definitely. While a few students were lucky enough to have ⁹*tuition fees / scholarships*, I didn't. I had to plan my spending carefully, so I had money for extras like ¹⁰*tuition fees / field trips*, and of course, occasionally enjoying myself too!

2 Complete the text with education collocations. Use the first letter to help you.

Last week, our class went to the local science museum. It was a good opportunity to ¹a_____ knowledge beyond the classroom, and I liked that we were encouraged to ²s_____ initiative and ³c_____ out research. We were ⁴a_____ on that and given a grade, and that motivated me more than having to ⁵m_____ details to pass a course. I felt like I was getting to know my subject ⁶i_____ out, but by actively doing something. I'm rubbish at ⁷c_____ for exams, but confident in presenting findings so I passed that course easily. Afterwards, we had to ⁸s_____ a report. It was a great experience overall, and fingers crossed that it'll help me ⁹s_____ a place in a future research project I'm interested in.

GRAMMAR 2

1 Choose the correct options to complete the text.

Personality science explores factors like genetics, environment, and culture and tries ¹*to uncover / uncovering* what makes people and societies different. But can we actually change our personality? Researchers at the University of California are beginning ²*to think / thinking* that we can, but that age and sustained effort are both key factors. One other area they will soon go on ³*to study / studying* is how societies could transform because of mass personality change caused by social media. Another question they are hoping ⁴*to answer / answering* is: how can we avoid ⁵*to raise / raising* a new generation who aren't affected by video games? Most would agree these topics are well worth studying and I would say that personality science deserves ⁶*to get / getting* more funding, because if not we risk not ⁷*to discover / discovering* all we need to. This wasn't a degree I knew about when I applied for university, so I think universities need to advertise more and encourage young people ⁸*to follow / following* this career path.

2 Rewrite the sentences using participle clauses.

1. This film, which was made for primary learners, explains tolerance really well.
2. He dislikes it when people are overly critical of his art.
3. Because he had been methodical throughout the project, he passed with an excellent grade.
4. The counsellor who offered careers advice was well liked by students.
5. It's important for you to listen to others.
6. Your upbringing is reported to affect your personality and also your mental health.
7. The film star was said to be very frugal, and never spent her earnings.
8. She grew up in a big family, so she was a very sociable person.
9. I admire people who meet deadlines.

VOCABULARY 2

1 Complete the dialogue with the words in the box. There are three extra words.

> conscientious extroverted idealistic
> impulsive introverts methodical
> obstinate placid tolerant

A: What type of person really makes a best friend?
B: I'm drawn to ¹_____. They tend to be more thoughtful in what they do, and plan everything step by step. They're more ²_____ and so probably won't cancel plans or forget your birthday. But I know an ³_____ friend can bring excitement to your life. They're more ⁴_____, they'll suggest last-minute adventures, things like that. It depends on what you're like, really.
A: That's very true. Some of my best friends are naturally ⁵_____, they bring calm and peace to stressful situations. Another crucial quality for me is being ⁶_____, reliable and considering how your actions affect others.

2 Complete the text using the correct form of the word in brackets.

Getting along with classmates during a project can be challenging, but it's far from ¹_____ (possible). Every group has the ²_____ (able) to get along and get the work done if there is good planning. If not, arguments can arise from the ³_____ (use) of time. Avoid this by focussing only on what's important to the project, distributing jobs and avoiding ⁴_____ (relevant) tasks. One common mistake is to ⁵_____ (estimate) what work needs to be done, meaning you have a huge amount to do as the deadline approaches. This can create unnecessary ⁶_____ (ease) and tension, and is when people can ⁷_____ (respect) each other by getting annoyed. One thing that's often ⁸_____ (rated) here is the power of calm. If you turn that on and ⁹_____ (activate) that feeling of stress, you'll get the job done better and more quickly.

REVIEW 2 UNITS 4–6

GRAMMAR 3

1 Write sentences which mean the same as the first.

1 Without his dad's help, he could never have afforded the festival tickets.
   Had _____.

2 I wish I had more money! I want to buy him a birthday cake.
   If I _____.

3 If you climbed that hill tonight, you would see the fireworks perfectly.
   Were _____.

4 You didn't tell me it was your graduation weekend, so I didn't bring a nice outfit.
   Had _____.

5 We need to get tickets now, before the concert sells out.
   Unless _____.

6 Coming by car? The centre of town is packed, avoid it!
   If you _____.

7 They didn't advertise the event, so not many people are here.
   If _____.

8 I'm terrible at making things, so I had to buy a fancy-dress costume!
   If _____.

9 I went to bed early so I missed the New Year countdown!
   If _____.

10 My advice is to visit the Edinburgh Festival in August.
   If _____.

SELF-ASSESSMENT!

2 Look back at your work in Units 4–6.
- ☐ passives review
- ☐ the causative
- ☐ gerunds and infinitives
- ☐ participle clauses
- ☐ conditionals review
- ☐ inverted conditionals

1 Tick ✓ the area of grammar that you feel most confident about.
2 (Circle) the area of grammar that you need to work on more.
3 Underline the area of grammar that you think you will use most in future.

VOCABULARY 3

1 Complete the text with the words and phrases in the box.

> break with tradition   falls in
> mark the occasion   milestone   rituals
> spectacles   transition   uphold traditions

University graduation is a significant ¹_____ in anyone's life, marking the ²_____ from academic life to the professional world. In many countries this typically ³_____ early summer and universities host a party or ceremony to ⁴_____. Graduation ceremonies in the UK are grand ⁵_____, complete with gowns, diplomas, and inspiring speeches. There are also ⁶_____ that ⁷_____, such as the tossing of caps in the air.
In some cases, modern students now have virtual graduations. While these changes ⁸_____, they allow everyone, no matter where their location, to celebrate.

2 Choose the correct words to complete the text.

In Rio de Janeiro, Brazil, carnival is the most ¹ *vibrant / customary* event of the year. The city's ² *atmospheric / festive* spirit shines brightly for a full week, so if you're looking for a ³ *vibrant / tranquil* holiday, this isn't the place to come. The streets come alive with ⁴ *flamboyant / raucous* costumes and decorations, creating a truly ⁵ *customary / atmospheric* setting that draws crowds from all round the world. ⁶ *Extravagant / Tranquil* parades run through the city, and live bands play ⁷ *raucous / flamboyant* tunes that keep everyone moving, and it's ⁸ *customary / extravagant* to get dressed up.

SELF-ASSESSMENT!

3 Look back at your work in Units 4–6.
- ☐ study and exams
- ☐ education – verbs and verb phrases
- ☐ personality
- ☐ negative prefixes
- ☐ celebrations
- ☐ describing celebrations

1 Tick ✓ the vocabulary group that had the most new words for you.
2 (Circle) the vocabulary group that you need to work on more.
3 Underline the vocabulary group that you think you will use most in future.

VOCABULARY REFERENCE 4-6

UNIT 4

academic year the months when you attend school
assignment a piece of work or job that you are given
deadline a time by which something must be done
dissertation a very long piece of writing done as part of a course
field trip a visit made by students to study something away from the school or university
finals exams taken at the end of a university course
plagiarism using another person's idea or work and pretending it is your own
scholarship the money given to a person by an organisation to pay for their education
student loan money that a student borrows from a bank to pay for their education
syllabus a plan showing the order of topics and/or books to be studied in a course
tuition fees the money that you pay to study
undergraduate a university student on a degree course
acquire knowledge to get or obtain the understanding you need
assess to decide the quality of something
carry out research to do an experiment or study
cram to force many things into a short time or space
drop out to stop attending a course before you finish
know your subject inside out to know everything about a subject/topic
memorise to learn something so you will remember it exactly
secure a place to be accepted onto a course
show initiative to use your own knowledge to do something without being told
submit an application to hand in a request

UNIT 5

conscientious showing care and effort in your duties
extrovert a person who enjoys being with others
extroverted describes a person who is outgoing and enjoys socialising
frugal careful with money or resources
idealistic believing that the world can be perfect
impulsive acting suddenly and without thinking about the consequences
insecure lacking confidence
introvert a person who tends to be quiet and prefers spending time alone rather than in large groups
introverted describes someone who enjoys solitude
methodical something who does things in an organised and systematic way
obstinate stubborn, refusing to change one's opinion
placid calm and not easily excited or upset
resolute someone who is determined and firm in why they are doing something
deactivate to stop a machine from operating
disrespect to show a lack of respect for someone/something
illegal not allowed by law
impossibility something that cannot happen or be done
inability the state of not being able to do something
irrelevant not related to what is being dicussed, etc.
misuse to use something in an incorrect way
overrated something considered to be better or more important than it really is
underestimate to consider something as being smaller/ less important than it really is
unease a feeling of discomfort or worry

UNIT 6

break with tradition do something differently than it has usually been done
come of age officially become an adult
fall on/in (a day/month) happen at a particular time
feast a large, special meal for many people
festivities activities to celebrate a special occasion
host a party organise and invite guests to a celebration
mark an occasion do something to show that an event is important
milestone an important event, step, or achievement
ritual a set of actions always performed in the same way, often as part of a ceremony
spectacle an exciting event for people to watch
transition a change from something to another
uphold a tradition do something special in the way It has always been done
atmospheric creating a special feeling or mood
customary traditional or usual
extravagant costing more than is necessary
festive suitable for a festival
flamboyant very bright or colourful, meant to be noticed
joyous bright and full of life or energy
raucous loud and maybe out of control
tranquil quiet and peaceful
vibrant bright and full of life or energy

DIGITAL CLASSROOM
PRACTICE EXTRA UNITS 4-6

UNIT 7 FUTUROLOGY

VOCABULARY

ADJECTIVES WITH DEPENDENT PROPOSITIONS

2 Complete the definitions with the correct words from Unit 7.

1 When something is _____ to something else, they are similar in size, amount or quality.
2 Being _____ to something means giving it a lot of time and energy.
3 If you are _____ by something, you have less opportunity to be successful.
4 To be _____ for something is to be unsuitable.
6 When something is _____ to something else, it is better than it.
7 If something is _____ to you, you cannot get it or use it.

READING

✓ EXAM TASK — READING AND USE OF ENGLISH PART 5

EXAM TIP
Read each paragraph quickly to get the main idea. Then, read the question but not the options. Read the paragraph quickly again and try to answer the question. Finally, check the options A–D and choose which best answers the question.

1 You are going to read an article about the flow state, in which the mind is totally absorbed in an activity. For questions 1–6, choose the answer (A, B, C or D) which you think fits best according to the text.

1 What does the writer say about Julia Christensen in the first paragraph?
  A She regrets giving up her old career.
  B Her primary interest is the effect of flow on dancers.
  C She is eager to experience the sensation of flow again.
  D Her writing about flow results from collaboration with others.

2 The word 'This' is used in line 22 to refer to the idea that
  A the state of rest is widely accepted as being necessary for happiness.
  B the view of happiness as hard to attain is unfounded.
  C an activity deliberately aimed at achieving happiness may be unsuccessful.
  D deep mental involvement is a key factor in feelings of happiness.

3 In the third paragraph, the writer is
  A explaining why the experience of flow is so desirable
  B challenging a common assumption about the experience of flow
  C evaluating the probability of experiencing flow when doing tasks
  D summarising factors that contribute to the experience of flow

4 What does the writer say about studies of flow in the fourth paragraph?
  A They have had highly conflicting results.
  B There is great enthusiasm for carrying them out.
  C Unusual methods of investigation have been used.
  D They are likely to have more success than previous ones.

5 What point does the writer make about the state of flow in the fifth paragraph?
  A Certain concepts related to it have become more accepted.
  B It is necessary for part of the brain to shut down for it to occur.
  C Investigations into its causes have used faulty equipment.
  D An explanation of the processes involved has been disputed.

6 In the final paragraph, the writer wants
  A to point out that the methods used to investigate flow need improvement
  B to justify the effort put into studies of one area of the brain's links to flow
  C to evaluate the benefits of further research into what causes flow
  D to question the validity of van der Linden's proposals about flow

Flow: the state of being so involved in an activity that nothing else matters

As a professional ballerina, Julia Christensen was familiar with what is known as the flow state: a total absorption in her body's movements, without the constant mental chatter that typically accompanies our waking lives. Little did she know that after an injury ended her ballet career, and she became a scientist, these experiences would go on to inform her work. Since then, she has explored the flow state, and a recent book charts her attempts to regain that blissful feeling of being fully immersed in an activity.

The psychologist Mihály Csíkszentmihalyi, who first coined the term, began his investigations into flow in the 1970s, when researching the question 'What is enjoyment?' After interviewing hundreds of participants about their lives, he found that their happiness peaks often occurred when high levels of mental focus were involved. The specific activity did not seem to matter, whether playing the violin or performing brain surgery, what counted was the feeling of immersion and mastery. 'The best moments,' he wrote, 'occur when a person's body or mind is stretched to its limits in a voluntary effort to accomplish something difficult and worthwhile.' **This** contradicts an assumption about happiness that is commonly held, with many believing it is gained from activities such as relaxing.

After further studies, Csíkszentmihalyi defined the core characteristics that lead to flow. In a nutshell, these are a high level of concentration, a sense of control, a decrease in worrying thoughts, a clear goal, and an accompanying lack of awareness of the minutes or hours flying by. According to his research, flow tends to occur when we find the perfect balance between our current abilities and the difficulty of the activity at hand. If a task is too easy, it fails to absorb our attention, we become distracted, and our thoughts wander. If it is too hard, we start to feel stressed by the task itself. It is only when we meet the sweet spot in between that we find the optimum level of engagement – and the pleasurable sensations that come with it.

Psychologists have designed a **questionnaire** that assesses the frequency of people's flow experiences to factors such as personality. They found that the more neurotic someone is, the less often flow occurs, perhaps because they struggle to turn off their inner critic, which could interfere with the state of heightened concentration. Our tendency to experience flow may be influenced by our DNA. A study comparing identical twins and non-identical twins indicated that genetic differences play a role. Exactly which genes are involved, and the underlying neural activity associated with flow, are still under scientific investigation. That's the holy grail, according to Christensen, with numerous scientists dedicated to understanding the physical basis of flow.

One theory has been that the flow state arises from reduced activity in the prefrontal regions of the brain, areas typically associated with 'higher-order thinking' and self-awareness. The idea was that you go into a form of autopilot without deliberating over every decision. A recent review, however, concludes that evidence for this theory is distinctly lacking, and experiments have reported contradictory results. This may be partly due to the practical challenges of achieving the flow state while using brain scanners, which tend to be very loud and distracting.

It may be a while before sufficient convincing evidence accumulates to explain the physical nature of flow. One researcher, Dimitri van der Linden, claims the experience of flow is related to an area in the brain stem called the *locus coeruleus*, which is widely connected to almost all other brain regions. It is also the main producer of the hormone and neurotransmitter noradrenaline, which helps to put us into a state of mental and physical arousal. Van der Linden argues that the flow state may arise when the locus coeruleus is moderately active. This allows it to raise our alertness and attention, so that the brain can respond quickly to incoming information, without us feeling overwhelmed and overstimulated. Van der Linden has published some tentative evidence for this idea, based on slightly artificial experiments in which participants played a complex memory game, while his team assessed the activity going on in their locus coeruleus regions. Sure enough, he found that people's feeling of flow corresponded with the expected activity. However, to avoid relying on artificially engineered laboratory tasks of this kind, and for more significant proof of flow's neural basis, many more studies of people performing their chosen activities in more natural settings where flow occurs will be vital. They are likely to have more success than previous ones.

2 **Emotional Intelligence** Have you ever experienced 'flow'? If so, what were you doing? If you haven't, what do you think might help you achieve it?

GRAMMAR

PLANS AND PREDICTIONS IN THE PAST

1 Order the sentences to make past predictions.

1 the train / would / be quicker, / I thought / but it wasn't.
2 but I'm happy / I didn't think / to see you / you'd come,
3 not a doctor. / become / imagined that / you would / become an actor, / I always
4 would be / people didn't / believe that / possible, / but it is / space travel
5 until it / I was / go out / started raining, / going to

2 Complete the text with the phrases in the box.

> didn't think you would   had assumed
> knew this would   thought you would
> wasn't going to   was going to

Thanks so much for helping with the project for my IT class. I ¹_____ start on my own until you called. To be honest, I ²_____ because I ³_____ that you were too busy to help. I know you're class president, and I ⁴_____ have too much to do. To be honest, I ⁵_____ work super hard, just enough to pass on this project, but I think we'll get a really good grade now. I ⁶_____ be easier with a partner. If you need help with maths, let me know!

3 Find and correct seven errors with past predictions.

In the 1950s, the television was an exciting piece of new technology. Some believe it would be a short-lived trend, but it quickly became clear that TV is going to stick around. It did, but many of their other predictions will turn out to be wrong. For example, many people believed that television will replace the radio and the cinema entirely. Although these are far less popular now than in the 50s, they are still going strong. Others were scared it were going to make books obsolete, but thankfully that didn't turn out to be true either. There were also people who think that TV was going to change how we spent our evenings forever, and no-one could contest that. What they didn't imagine at all, however, is that we are going to have a TV screen that fit in our pocket. That was pure science fiction back then!

FUTURE CONTINUOUS AND FUTURE PERFECT

4 Are these time phrases usually used with future perfect (FP), future continuous (FC), or both (B)?

1 By 2050, ...
2 At 9 o'clock tomorrow, ...
3 In five years' time, ...
4 Tomorrow morning, ...
5 This time next week, ...
6 In two weeks' time, ...
7 By this time next year, ...

5 Write sentences using the time phrases in Exercise 4.

6 Complete the text in the future perfect or future continuous form of the verb in brackets.

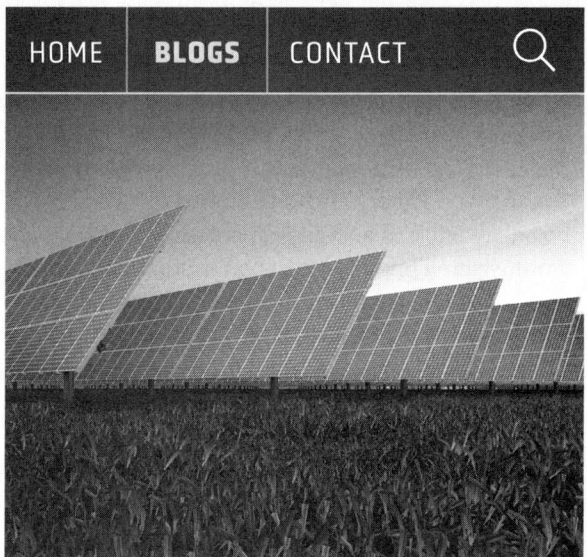

Solar power use is rising. By 2030, many say we ¹_____ (integrate) solar energy into our lives, transforming how we power our gadgets.

By the time you've read this article, someone somewhere ²_____ (install) solar panels on their roof, allowing them to power their house using renewable energy. However, the big change in how we use solar will be in chargers. Very soon, we ³_____ (use) solar-powered chargers every day for mobiles, laptops and electric bikes. As solar technology advances and demand rises, manufacturers ⁴_____ (focus) on how efficient solar-powered mobile chargers are. It is feasible to imagine that by next year, companies ⁵_____ (develop) solar chargers that charge mobiles twice as fast as now. Soon, solar power ⁶_____ (become) an integral part of modern living.

62 | UNIT 7 FUTUROLOGY

READING AND USE OF ENGLISH

EXAM TASK — READING AND USE OF ENGLISH PART 2

1 For questions 1–8, read the text below and think of the word which best fits each gap. Use only one word in each gap. There is an example at the beginning (0).

THE VALUE OF WIND POWER

It ⁰ __was__ a Scottish engineer, James Blyth, who invented the first wind-powered electrical generator. In 1887, he built a windmill attached to a dynamo to capture energy to light his cottage. He even succeeded ¹_____ storing the power in a battery invented by the French engineer Camille Alphonse Faure. Blyth was ²_____ of his time, arguing that wind power was good for the environment and cheaper than fossil fuels, and dreaming of a future in which every house ³_____ be powered by a wind turbine.

Now with the pressing threat of climate change, most countries are trying to reduce their carbon emissions, and the construction of wind power turbines is ⁴_____ the increase. For countries ⁵_____ wind power is a viable option, it is likely that thousands more wind turbines will have ⁶_____ built before the mid-twenty-first century. However, as wind power technology develops, the total number of turbines under construction will probably start to ⁷_____ down, with fewer, larger turbines that can generate power more efficiently taking ⁸_____ place of smaller ones.

VOCABULARY

IDIOMS

1 Complete the sentences with one word.

1 Online class is the _____ of both worlds: your classmates but no travel time.
2 I forgot my homework, so I'll need to _____ the music in class later.
3 Learning and curiosity go hand in _____.
4 My brother can be a _____ in the neck sometimes!
5 Saving money is easier said _____ done.
6 _____ a nutshell, AI has changed the world.
7 I need to set the record _____ – it was me who broke your laptop.
8 Don't take adverts at _____ value, always read the small print.
9 People often turn a blind _____ to where their clothes come from.

2 Complete the conversation with idioms from Exercise 1.

Joe: You know, I've been thinking about travelling to work by bus instead of driving. With the high petrol prices and climate crisis news, I want to make a change.

Amina: Yeah, in theory, it sounds great, but it's ¹_____. I'm not sure I could give up my car. When buses are late it's such ²_____.

Joe: True, but if more people switched, the bus system would improve. They ³_____, don't they?

Amina: I guess, and if we continue driving our own cars, we'll have to ⁴_____ and accept that we'll have more pollution. Public transport is a much better choice, even though it isn't perfect. People tend to ⁵_____ the problems of using cars because they like the convenience.

Joe: I know. ⁶_____, there isn't a perfect way to get around, but we have to make hard choices if we want to be green.

Amina: True. I've also read about car-pooling, where you share a car. It's ⁷_____ if you can get used to it.

UNIT 7 FUTUROLOGY

LISTENING

1 Read the questions below quickly. Imagine what each extract will be about. Match the photos (A–C) to the listening extracts (1–3).

2 Match the words and phrases from the listening extracts to the definitions. Then listen and check your answers.

1 to be over the moon
2 to conjure up (phrasal verb)
3 executive assistant
4 fortune teller

a a person you pay to tell you what they think will happen in the future
b to make a picture or idea appear in your mind, like magic
c to be very pleased
d a person whose job is to help an important manager with their work

EXAM TIP

Listen to the whole extract before choosing your answers. Use the second listening to confirm if your choices are correct.

✓ EXAM TASK LISTENING PART 1

3 🔊 7.1 You will hear three different extracts. For questions 1–6, choose the answer (A, B or C) which fits best according to what you hear. There are two questions for each extract.

Extract One

You hear two friends talking about some predictions they made about music earlier in the year.

1 How does the woman feel about her prediction about the band Hothead?
 A uncertain how she was so accurate
 B delighted to feel superior to experts
 C surprised other people thought differently

2 Why does the man mention Hothead's drummer?
 A to indicate his surprise at the current situation
 B to explain why he's unsure what will happen next
 C to clarify the prediction he'd made originally

Extract Two

You hear part of a discussion programme about AI.

3 The woman is optimistic about the use of AI for clothes shopping because she
 A expects people to appreciate the convenience.
 B suspects that people have a desire to be adventurous.
 C believes many people currently have difficulty making decisions.

4 What opinion do they both express about AI?
 A There will be plenty of opposition to it.
 B There is no basis to many of the worries about it.
 C There will be good reason for acceptance of it.

Extract Three

You hear two friends talking about their lives.

5 What do they both say about the future?
 A It's important to make plans for it.
 B It's natural to be concerned about it.
 C It's foolish to focus on it excessively.

6 What does the man say about the job he left?
 A He regrets the fact that he ever applied for it.
 B He thinks he misunderstood what it would be like.
 C He feels that having it benefitted him in certain ways.

WRITING

A STORY

1. Do you like reading or listening to personal experience stories? What makes a personal story interesting?

2. Choose the two most common ways that personal experience stories end.
   1. With a twist or surprise, e.g. *Suddenly, another person arrived and ...*
   2. By asking a question, e.g. *Has that ever happened to you? Tell us!*
   3. By sharing what the experience made you think, e.g. *That experience really made me think about ...*
   4. With a short sentence describing the moral of the story, e.g. *As you can see, planning is important!*

3. Complete the table with the phrases in the box.

   > My day was going normally, until ...
   > After that day, I learned to never ...
   > When I look back on that day now, I feel ...
   > What that taught me was ...
   > Although I had expected to ...
   > We all assumed that we would ...
   > Next time, I'll be sure to ...
   > I had planned not to go out, but then ...
   > As you can see, X is important. If not ...

Starting a personal experience story	Ending a personal experience story

4. Think about a time in your life when you expected something to be a bad experience, but it was better than you expected. Make notes on the points:
   1. What made this experience interesting.
   2. Why you expected the experience to be bad.
   3. What you were feeling before the experience.
   4. What went differently from what you expected.
   5. What you feel about the experience now.

5. Plan the structure of your personal experience. Look at your notes from Exercise 4, decide in which paragraph they should be included.

1	Start	
2	Paragraph 1	
3	Paragraph 2	
4	Conclusion	

6. Write your personal experience story in 220–260 words.

SELF-EVALUATION

Check your writing:

Content: Have you started your story with a sentence showing you changed your mind about the experience? Does the rest of the story explain why? Does the end show why the story is important to you? ☹ ☺ 😐 😊

Communication: Are the events of your story clear to the reader? Is your personal experience story interesting? ☹ ☺ 😐 😊

Organisation: Is the text well-organised and linked? Is there a good flow of ideas? ☹ ☺ 😐 😊

Language: Have you used a variety of structures and vocabulary? Have you included some new language from this unit? ☹ ☺ 😐 😊

SPEAKING AT A PUBLIC MEETING

1 PLANNING

I'm going to attend a public meeting about: _____

I'm working in group number _____ , who are:
_____

We want:
_____

TIP When another group gives a counterargument to what you said, be ready with a 'You may say that, but …' response.

2 SPEAK AT AN APPROPRIATE PACE AND USE PAUSES

Why is pace important?
_____
_____
_____

Why are pauses effective?
_____
_____
_____

Where in your anecdote could you pause?

3 USE RHETORICAL DEVICES

A short list of what we want:
_____
_____
_____
_____
_____

What personal anecdote could I tell to make my argument strong?
_____
_____
_____
_____
_____
_____

What key words do we want to repeat to make our point strong?
_____
_____
_____

4 MAINTAINING A CONFIDENT POSTURE

ORACY 4

💼 **Communication** It's good to think about posture because …

_____
_____
_____

🚩 **TIP** Practise telling your anecdote with another person in your group. Ask them to respond as if they were the other group.

When I practised my anecdote, my posture was …

_____

During the meeting, make notes in this table.

My classmate _____	
Did your classmate play their role well?	
Did your classmate use any rhetorical techniques?	
Did your classmate speak at an appropriate pace, and use pauses?	
Did your classmate use a confident posture?	

After the discussion:

I talked to my classmate _____ about what he/she contributed, and she/he gave me feedback. I need to think more about …

_____
_____
_____

SELF-EVALUATION

I can …
- use appropriate rhetorical devices. ○
- maintain a confident posture. ○
- speak at an appropriate pace and use pauses. ○

UNIT 7 FUTUROLOGY | 67

UNIT 8 WILD PLANET

VOCABULARY

ADJECTIVES WITH PREFIXES

1 Complete the adjectives using a prefix from the box. Sometimes, more than one answer is possible.

| anti- | de | hyper | mid | non- | over |
| post | pre- | re | semi- | ultra- | under |

1 _____ claimed/wilded
2 _____ critical/active
3 _____ violent/profit
4 _____ week/year
5 _____ nuclear/nationalist
6 _____ commissioned/valued
7 _____ war/colonial
8 _____ funded/developed
9 _____ permanent/wild
10 _____ used/developed
11 _____ industrial/arranged
12 _____ expensive/careful

2 Complete the sentences with adjectives with prefixes from Exercise 1.

1 Plastic is still _____ these days, and the fight to use less continues.
2 In countries like Peru, _____ industrialisation led to deforestation.
3 In the _____ era, communities relied more on nature.
4 Many birds are returning to former farmlands that have been _____.
5 Some _____ hotels have beautiful views, but so do many cheap campsites.

READING AND USE OF ENGLISH

✓ EXAM TASK   READING AND USE OF ENGLISH PART 3

1 For questions 1–8, read the text below. Use the word given in capitals at the end of some of the lines to form a word that fits in the gap in the same line. There is an example at the beginning (0).

Horses prove they can plan for the future

The English ⁰ _saying_ 'you can lead a horse to water, but you can't make it drink' has been used for centuries to describe the difficulty of getting someone to act in their own best interests. However, new research suggests this phrase has been ¹ _____ used to suggest that horses have low ² _____. In a study by ³ _____ at Nottingham Trent University, researchers analysed the ⁴ _____ of horses in a reward-based game. The game involved food rewards with the rules changing slightly from one stage to another as they progressed. The horses showed the ability to plan ahead ⁵ _____ as the rules changed, and, in order to get the most food treats possible, adapted their ⁶ _____. Previous research had suggested that horses cannot proactively think ahead, whereas this study found that they have ⁷ _____ of how their actions affect future outcomes. Lead researcher, Louise Evans, advises those who train horses to note the benefits of rewards for improving ⁸ _____ compared to punishments.

SAY

FAIR/INTELLIGENT
SCIENCE
RESPOND

SUCCEED
BEHAVE

AWARE

PERFORM

READING

✓ EXAM TASK   READING AND USE OF ENGLISH PART 7

1 You are going to read an extract from a magazine article. Six paragraphs have been removed from the extract. Choose from the paragraphs A–G the one which fits each gap (1–6). There is one extra paragraph which you do not need to use.

EXAM TIP

If you are taking a long time on one gap, move on and come back to it at the end. There will be fewer choices then.

Saving baby sea turtles

Turtles are an endangered species and their favourite nesting spots in Sri Lanka are coming under pressure from development, poaching and tourists. Fortunately, volunteers are stepping in to help.

On a sweltering night on Sri Lanka's western coast, there's a flurry of activity. Several young people in orange hi-vis vests are squatting in a circle on the beach, digging in the sand in semi-darkness. The team of volunteers patrol a popular tourist beach, scouting for turtle nesting sites. Finding the nests can require a bit of detective work.

[1]

The purpose of this is to look for eggs. Turtle eggs have long been poached as a food source by coastal communities, but more recently it is human activity of another kind that has proved a greater threat. As the capital city Colombo has sprawled, especially during the past decade, restaurants and other tourist amenities have mushroomed, bringing in more people.

[2]

Examples like this illustrate why life is becoming more difficult for the turtles and have caused the volunteering group to expand their activities to include regular patrols. Working with the coastguard, the volunteers help find eggs laid in risky areas and remove them to safer nesting places on the beach until they hatch. Even if they emerge from their eggs during the day, the turtles usually head for the sea once it is cooler and darker. These juveniles are given safe passage by night-time patrols.

[3]

The reason for their unhappiness may be that they were poachers. Poachers pose a significant threat to the five species of sea turtles – olive ridleys, green turtles, leatherbacks, hawksbills and loggerheads – which nest on Sri Lanka's beaches. Capturing, killing, injuring or possessing sea turtles or their eggs is an offence under Sri Lankan law.

[4]

One way of doing this is to inform people about the problems and the solutions by holding awareness sessions. About 90% of the villagers in the area now support the turtle conservation efforts after attending them. However, there still remain a minority of people who are involved in poaching eggs to sell.

[5]

Such a solution is a great way of making part of the problem part of the solution. However, another problem is the existence of illegal 'turtle hatcheries' that operate in Sri Lanka's tourist areas. Here, turtle eggs poached from the beaches are kept until they hatch. Naïve tourists believing they are doing good, buy the juvenile turtles after hatching to be released into the ocean, even though this is against the law and harmful to them.

[6]

Tourists clearly need to be better-educated about the damage their well-intentioned behaviour can have. Meanwhile, as the sun goes down, and the moon rises, hundreds of turtles begin to crawl across the beach to the water, while music blasts out from one of the many nearby beach restaurants. For the volunteers, it's great to see the hatchlings entering the ocean, knowing they have helped it to happen.

A An occurrence of this kind would mean that these tiny turtles the size of a baby's palm would struggle to emerge from beneath the sand as they hatched. It would be a tragedy if these little creatures never got their first glimpse of the world as a result of human behaviour.

B The search involves scouting for turtle tracks and then following the trail, Vikasitha Liyanage tells me. She is a member of a local environmentalist group who patrol between 9.30 pm and 2 am, and sometimes dig holes on the beach.

C Nevertheless, some who hunt the nests are not deterred by this, since certain restaurants and hotels buy the eggs to sell to foreigners as an exotic food, at a premium price. Turtle eggs are now in great commercial demand, so patrolling needs to be combined with educating both coastal communities and tourists.

D This is because coming into contact with humans in this way can transfer germs to them, and being let out into the waters in small numbers, during daylight, reduces their chances of survival. It means predators such as seabirds or larger fish can easily spot them.

E Not everyone is happy about these activities though, and the group have to be aware of the dangers. Once while guarding the turtles, a volunteer tells me they had an encounter with some very agitated people with dogs, who were trying to stop what they were doing.

F A further step that has been taken to encourage them to change their ways is that of recruiting them to protect nests themselves, thus providing an alternative income. In the southern part of the island, the Turtle Conservation Project has recruited local people to patrol the beach around the clock.

G Along with these developments come parties, booming music, and much plastic and chemical waste, all of which disrupts turtle nesting during the breeding season, from November to April. A restaurant manager says he has seen for himself how crowds with flashlights and cameras disturb turtles arriving to lay eggs, making them return to the sea instead.

GRAMMAR

REPORTED SPEECH – STRUCTURES WITH *THAT*

1 Rewrite the sentences in reported speech. Use the verb in brackets.

1. Girl: When are we going to the nature reserve? (ask)
2. Dad: We've booked for Sunday afternoon. (reply)
3. Girl: Do you think we can touch the animals? (ask)
4. Dad: No, we won't. It'll be like the photos on their webpage? (tell)
5. Girl: I remember seeing that, it's like a safari. (said)

2 Choose the correct options.

1. He agreed *with / to* me that the wildlife reserve was a fantastic day trip.
2. The biologist pointed *out that / me out that* the wetlands were crucial for birds.
3. The council *promised / promised to* local residents that they would expand the conservation area.
4. The guide said *us that / that* he would show us the hidden trails.
5. The park ranger reminded *that / us that* we needed to stay on the paths.
6. The report revealed *us that / to us that* the forest's biodiversity had improved.
7. A child shouted *that / us that* they had spotted a deer in the distance.
8. The ranger warned *us / to us* that noise could disturb the animals.

3 Rewrite the sentences from a museum visitor book with the more formal *to* infinitive instead of *that* after a reporting verb. Use the subject and verb in brackets.

1. 'The museum's exhibit on endangered species was very informative.' (one visitor/find)
2. 'I'm a history professor and the fossil collection is the best in the country.' (an educator/think)
3. 'The museum's interactive section on climate change is a must.' (a school group/consider)
4. 'The section on prehistoric plant life is fascinating!' (our group/find)
5. 'I think the new exhibit on ocean habitats is the best addition.' (a local resident/consider)
6. 'The museum's portrayal of extinct species is a sad reminder of human impact on wildlife.' (one visitor/feel)

REPORTED SPEECH – STRUCTURES WITHOUT *THAT*

4 Choose the correct options.

1. The vet advised the farmer *to check / checking* the water source for disease.
2. The zoo denied *to mistreat / mistreating* the animals.
3. The government decided *not to allow / not allowing* animals in circus performances.
4. The vet recommended *to bring / bringing* the cat to her surgery.
5. The animal activist refused *to support / supporting* the fur industry.
6. The government warned people *not to travel / not travelling* without a malaria vaccine.
7. The poacher admitted *to hunt / hunting* illegally.

5 Complete the conversation with the correct form of the verbs in brackets.

Manager: Welcome to the animal shelter! We're glad you ¹_____ (decide) to volunteer.

Volunteer: Thank you for ²_____ (agree) to let me help! I'm so happy my teacher ³_____ (advise) me to look you up. I'm ⁴_____ (consider) applying to study veterinary science, and he ⁵_____ (tell) me to get some experience first. Plus, I love animals, of course!

Manager: No problem at all. So, let's get into it. I ⁶_____ (recommend) starting by cleaning the cat bedding area. It's a great way to get to know them.

Volunteer: OK, great. I need to ⁷_____ (persuade) them to come out with food, right? Last night my cat ⁸_____ (refuse) to move from my chair until I gave her food!

Manager: Good point! Let's go and do it together.

6 Rewrite the parts of the text in bold with an impersonal reporting structure.

> ¹**According to estimates**, around 50% of UK households have pets, but this figure drops for retired people. However, ²**people say that** having an animal at home can greatly improve physical activity in the elderly, and also provide companionship. In addition, ³**researchers claim that** these animal friendships improve mood and reduce loneliness. That's why some elderly care homes are now pet-friendly. In fact, ⁴**many people believe that** that over 50% are. Some hospitals are also trialing pet visits to help improve patient mood, so next time you visit an in-patient, don't be surprised to see their cat there too. Of course, ⁵**nobody expects that** all UK hospitals will have pet visits in future, but many will! ⁶**Researchers predict that** this trend will spread to other countries too. What do you think? Leave a comment below.

7 Rewrite the sentence so that it means the same as the first. Use between two and six words.

1 Researchers believe that veganism will increase over the next ten years. **(BELIEVED)**
   It _____ veganism will increase over the next ten years.
2 'I think *Charlotte's Web* is the best book about animals,' she said. **(CONSIDERED)**
   She _____ be the best book about animals.
3 'I'd love to have a pet!' he said. **(MENTIONED)**
   He _____ love to have a pet.
4 'I'm the most experienced horse-rider here,' said the girl. **(CLAIMED)**
   The girl _____ was the most experienced horse-rider there.
5 'Don't put your hand in the animal cages!' said the zoo keeper. **(WARNED)**
   The zoo keeper _____ put our hands in the animal cages.

VOCABULARY

THE ANIMAL KINGDOM

1 Complete the sentences with words from Unit 8. Use the first letter to help you.

1 Most **m**_____ life, reptiles and insects are **c**_____ **b**_____.
2 All **m**_____, such as humans, are **w**_____ **b**_____.
3 Although domesticated, cats are **f**_____ **p**_____, while mice and rats are their **p**_____.
4 The annual **m**_____ route of zebra is changing because their **n**_____ **h**_____ is changing.
5 The zoo's tigers, despite being raised **i**_____ **c**_____, still retained their **s**_____ nature.

2 Complete the text using words from Exercise 1.

> Climate change is rapidly changing the ¹_____ _____ of all animal life on earth, from ²_____ reptiles to ³_____.
>
> One of the most visible impacts of this is on ⁴_____ patterns. Many birds are arriving too early or too late to find the resources they depend on. This also means their ⁵_____ must adapt to survive. As ecosystems break down, some animals even face extinction, such as the white rhino. To prevent this, these animals are being kept ⁶_____ _____.
>
> ⁷_____ life is at risk too. Warmer oceans push fish and plankton further from the equator, affecting the food chain. ⁸_____ such as sharks also move into new territories, upsetting established ecosystems. These warmer waters also contribute to the ice caps melting, and thus polar bears suffer. These ⁹_____ predators are now struggling to survive.

LISTENING

1 Match the words in bold in the sentences 1–5 to the photos A–E.

1. A shark **fin** appeared, about three metres away.
2. Loads of visitors were in the viewing area, waiting for spectacular pictures of bears **feeding**.
3. Bison have been known to **charge** anything they see as a threat.
4. This bull, a creature known for its huge size, remained soundless, softly **munching** away on leaves.
5. One day, while walking my dog through the **bush**, I saw a boomer – a male kangaroo.

EXAM TASK — LISTENING PART 4

2 🔊 8.1 You will hear five short extracts in which people are talking about an experience they had involving a wild animal. While you listen, you must complete both tasks.

EXAM TIP
Some people do both tasks simultaneously, and others do Task 1 on the first listen and task 2 on the second listen. Try out both strategies and decide what works best for you.

TASK ONE

For questions 1–5, choose from the list (A–H) how each speaker says they felt during their experience with a wild animal.

A keen to repeat it
B overwhelmed by its beauty
C confused about what was happening
D eager to move away
E terrified to be so close
F determined to get a photo
G calm and in control
H reassured by some information

Speaker 1 [1]
Speaker 2 [2]
Speaker 3 [3]
Speaker 4 [4]
Speaker 5 [5]

TASK TWO

For questions 6–10, choose from the list (A–H) what the speaker says was surprising about their experience.

A how aggressive the animal looked
B how easy it was to deceive the animal
C how quiet the animal was
D how other people reacted to their story
E how slowly time seemed to pass
F how many details they noticed
G how large the animal appeared
H how other people failed to follow advice

Speaker 1 [6]
Speaker 2 [7]
Speaker 3 [8]
Speaker 4 [9]
Speaker 5 [10]

3 **Critical Thinking** Do you think there are enough regulations in place to protect wild animals in your country? What could be done to improve them?

WRITING

A REPORT

1 How do people feel about the natural environment in your area? Do you think it needs to be improved? Why? / Why not?

2 Choose the correct option to complete the sentences about reports.

1. The language in reports is usually quite *formal / informal*.
2. The person reading this report *will / won't* know some basic information about your local area.
3. A report to the local council *should / shouldn't* start with *Dear Councillor*.
4. Reports *usually / never* have headings for each section.
5. This task asks you to write about *what you think / what people in your town think*.
6. A report talks about the *past and present / the past, present and hypothetical future*.

3 Read the exam task and plan your report. Make notes for each paragraph.

1	Introduction (reason for writing, topic)	
Paragraph 2 heading		
2	Local peoples' negative and/or positive opinions	
Paragraph 3 heading		
3	Mention possible improvements	
4	Conclusion (summary, what you want to happen)	

EXAM TASK — WRITING PART 2

You recently conducted a survey into how people in your town feel about the natural environment there, and what they would like to see done to improve it. You have been asked to write a report for the local council about your findings.

In your report, you should summarise what you learnt from the survey about how local people feel about the natural environment and outline their suggestions for how they would like to see it improved.

4 Write your report in 220–260 words.

SELF-EVALUATION

Check your writing:

Content: Have you covered all the points asked for? What did the survey say? What improvements did you ask for, and why?

Communication: Can the reader clearly understand the survey results and local people's opinions? Is the style appropriate for a report?

Organisation: Is the text well-organised and linked? Is there a good flow of ideas?

Language: Have you used a variety of structures and vocabulary? Have you included some new language from this unit?

EXAM TIP

In your report, use a variety of modal verbs to make recommendations.

A SCHOOL PLEDGE

1 GETTING STARTED

How can we work together to amplify change?

My partner is:
_____

Some ways in which little things add up to bigger things are …
_____
_____
_____

TIP Look at local online newspapers to find examples of collective action in your area.

2 THINK

We think it's better to work in a group when you …
_____
_____

We feel it's good to work alone when …
_____
_____

Example of collective action	1	2	3
How did it have an impact?			

How would this collective action have been different if just one person was doing it?

3 EXPLORE

My group is …

We want to make our school more sustainable. Ways of encouraging others to join us are:
_____
_____
_____

Draw a star by the things that would work best if people used collective action for them.

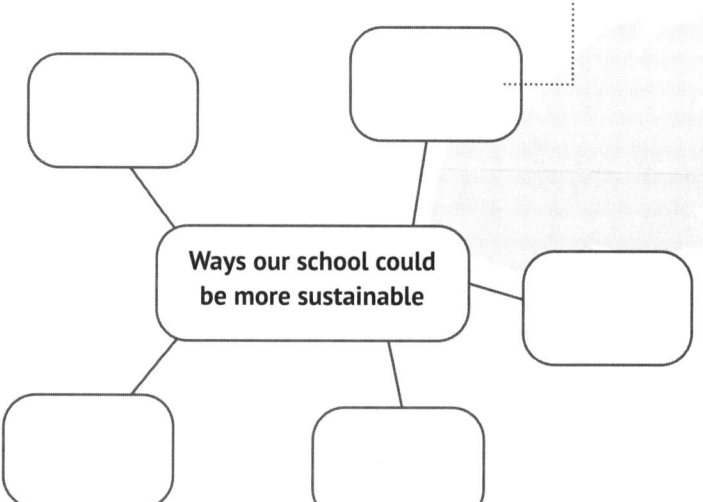

Ways our school could be more sustainable

UNIT 8 WILD PLANET

4 DEVELOP

EXPLORING SUSTAINABILITY 4

Our best two/three ideas are:
_____
_____
_____

Our sustainability pledge:
_____
_____
_____
_____

In future, how will you measure the positive impact of these things?

Plan your pledge video

Where will you film it?
_____
_____

My role in making the video?
_____

What will make it engaging?
_____
_____
_____

Some synonyms and paraphrases of 'We pledge to …' are:
_____
_____
_____

5 PRESENT

TIP — **Digital Literacy**
Pledge videos can be more engaging when they contain different scenes and speakers. Consider using pauses between scenes or splicing several videos together to create a final product.

- Is our video easy to understand?
- Is it engaging?
- Does it contain all the information we want?

I watched the other pledge videos and I thought that the one most likely to succeed was … because…

Does everyone know what they're doing?
Do we know which order we're presenting in?
Have we got everything we need?

After the presentation

Things we did well:
_____
_____
_____

Things we could improve:
_____
_____
_____

SELF-EVALUATION

I can …
- recognise the potential for collective action to enact and amplify change. ○
- identify, gather and organise relevant information. ○
- write a sustainability pledge. ○
- work constructively in a group video task. ○

UNIT 9 TRAVEL BUG

VOCABULARY

TRAVEL – COLLOCATIONS AND PHRASES

1 Complete the sentences with travel collocations and phrases from Unit 9.

1. After we arrive in Rome, we'll _____ like the Colosseum and the Vatican City.
2. Our plans for the trip _____ when the train was cancelled.
3. We're looking forward to relaxing and _____ on our holiday.
4. The _____ offered unlimited food, drinks, and activities.
5. The celebrity took a _____ to a private island.
6. _____ was enough for us, as we wanted to explore the local restaurants in the evening.
7. On the way to the pyramids, let's _____ in Cairo and explore the city for a day.
8. We booked a _____ to Cancun that included flights, accommodation, and excursions.
9. We stayed in _____ so we could cook our own meals.
10. After years of dreaming and saving, we finally booked our _____ to go to Mount Everest!
11. My ideal holiday is with a _____ option. It's so relaxing not to have to think about cooking!
12. Due to high winds, all _____ flights have been delayed. Check the board for more information.

READING AND USE OF ENGLISH

✓ EXAM TASK READING AND USE OF ENGLISH PART 1

1 For questions 1–8, read the text below and decide which answer (A, B, C or D) best fits each gap. There is an example at the beginning (0).

WORKING IN THE HOTEL INDUSTRY

As the General Manager of a beach resort hotel, I'm privileged to be part of an industry dedicated to **0** _crafting_ the holiday of a lifetime for our guests. Not only do we provide quality accommodation, but we also offer unforgettable experiences that leave **1**_____ memories. Whether guests are on an all-inclusive package holiday or **2**_____ for a self-catering stay, our **3**_____ is to go above and beyond in making their visit extraordinary. From orchestrating breathtaking weddings to arranging special outings that **4**_____ guests to see the sights or simply get away from it all, we **5**_____ pride in turning dreams into reality. Every day is filled with new challenges – it's not all **6**_____ sailing ensuring that our guests' needs are met, but we always go the extra mile to do so. Best of all are the warm connections **7**_____ between members of the hotel staff and our visitors, who come from all **8**_____ of life and numerous different cultures.

0	**A** crafting	**B** tuning
	C forming	**D** fitting
1	**A** constant	**B** lasting
	C steady	**D** lengthy
2	**A** choosing	**B** selecting
	C preferring	**D** opting
3	**A** assignment	**B** project
	C mission	**D** operation
4	**A** provide	**B** allow
	C offer	**D** present
5	**A** put	**B** set
	C take	**D** make
6	**A** plain	**B** simple
	C basic	**D** common
7	**A** joined	**B** united
	C shaped	**D** formed
8	**A** kinds	**B** walks
	C turns	**D** places

READING

EXAM TASK — READING AND USE OF ENGLISH PART 8

1 You are going to read an article about Antarctica. For questions 1–10, choose from the sections (A–E). The sections may be chosen more than once. In which section are the following found?

a desire to influence how Antarctica is thought of	1
a description of how being in Antarctica can affect a person's sense of their own size	2
details of a particular type of environmental impact caused by an individual visitor to Antarctica	3
a feature of Antarctica that people can experience without visiting	4
the idea that being unable to visit Antarctica makes the desire to go stronger	5
a quote in praise of Antarctica's unique perfection	6
someone's decision to purposefully avoid visiting Antarctica	7
the difficulty of conveying the wonder of Antarctica	8
information about professionals from contrasting backgrounds educating others about Antarctica	9
a claim that creative acts might be more persuasive in saving Antarctica from harm	10

Antarctica

As visitor numbers grow, so does the environmental impact

A After one trip to the continent of Antarctica, the Australian broadcaster Andrew Denton declared that if it were music, it would be Mozart, or if literature, Shakespeare. He also said that 'it is something even greater; the only place on Earth that is still as it should be. May we never tame it.' Yet, with sea ice cover continually dropping, the Antarctic is not as it should be. It is ironic that the more people visit it, the more they feel a passion to protect it. And every person who goes there contributes to its destruction. It is estimated that the average carbon emissions for an Antarctic tourist are 3.76 tonnes – roughly what a person typically generates in an entire year.

B The port of Hobart in Tasmania is Australia's gateway to Antarctica. On the waterfront is Hobartica, part of the Beaker Street science and art festival that takes place yearly. Its founder Dr Margo Adler has never been to Antarctica – but this has been a deliberate choice. 'I've always been really fascinated, but I don't really have a good justification for going,' she says. Through artistic endeavours, she hopes people can get a kind of access to it, and declares that she wants people to view Antarctica as an incredible place that we should protect and appreciate, but not as somewhere they need to visit themselves. According to Adler, the people who do go to Antarctica can say, 'This place is pristine. We need to keep it that way. But let me tell you about it'

C Hobartica features visual and sound art inspired by the continent, talks by artists and scientists, Finnish sauna tents and a unique Antarctic icy plunge pool: participants enter water that matches the temperature of Antarctic water that day, then move to water matched to the predicted temperature in 2050. As a scientist Adler wants to raise awareness about Antarctica, but so do many artists. With similar aims, creative people have long visited Antarctica on residencies allowing them to work there for a time. This has inspired novels, paintings etc… that draw attention to aspects of the continent.

D The children's author Alison Lester has been to Antarctica five times so far, and says it is like nowhere else: 'It's almost like going to outer space in that when you're down there, you're so insignificant and part of such a huge, pristine world. And I guess, because it's so inaccessible, there's always that thing: if you can't do something, you want to do it more!' Lester believes that the arts have the best chance of getting the message of conservation across to the public: there is value in not going yourself. 'The more people know about it, the more they will grow to love it and they will want to protect it, and I think that's what the arts can do, in a way that science often can't do.'

E Philip Samartzis, a sound artist whose work is featured in Hobartica, has been to Antarctica to document the industrial sounds of station life the famous wind. He says he's seen a shift in the focus of artists who visit in recent years towards questions around gender equality, the ethics of being there, and the impact we have on the last pristine wilderness environment in the world. Elizabeth Leane is a professor of Antarctic studies and has been to the continent six times. 'It's astonishingly beautiful, and it's a real dilemma, in the sense that I want everyone to be able to see what I've seen, because it's spectacular. It's hard to put into words.' Leane adds that after reading literature about it, she has come to the conclusion that not only can you write an excellent novel about Antarctica without going there, you can also write a terrible one when you have.

GRAMMAR

INVERSION FOR EMPHASIS

1 Choose the correct words to complete the conversation.

Saoirse: You know, I had such a good spring holiday. [1] *Little / Less* did I think that having no money wouldn't matter that much!

Clara: Really? Under no circumstances [2] *would I / I would* give up my annual holiday abroad. I need a change of scene every so often.

Saoirse: I got a change, I just didn't go far! [3] *Not until / Not only* I took my road trip did I realise how stunningly diverse the countryside was. Seriously, [4] *never / little* have I appreciated Scotland more!

Clara: You've got a point. Until last year I'd never been to the Western Isles. Not only did I spend less than I would've on a package holiday, [5] *but / than* it was green travel too, and I learned loads. [6] *Only after / No sooner* I got there did I realise how little I knew about Viking history.

Saoirse: Yes, there's so much to learn. Never [7] *did / had* I expect to say this, but I think I'll plan a trip to the islands next year. Fancy coming?

2 Rewrite the sentences so that they start with the word or phrase in (brackets).

1 We really didn't know that our detour through the countryside would take us to such an amazing village. (little)
2 It was only when I travelled solo that I discovered how much I enjoyed my own company. (only)
3 It's extremely important not to forget your passport when travelling by plane. (under no)
4 I saw such a stunning sunset in Sydney. I hadn't seen one like that before. (never)
5 I only started to calm down after the plane had landed. (only)
6 I got the confirmation email, then right away I realised I'd put in the wrong dates! (no sooner)

3 Find and correct seven mistakes with inversion for emphasis.

Had I never I imagined that being a location scout for the movie industry would be so thrilling. Not only it involves travelling to the most stunning and hidden places, but also discovering gems that even locals often overlook. Hardly had I started the job but I realised how demanding it could be, balancing tight deadlines with finding the perfect backdrop for a director's vision.

Rarely we get to relax, as every shoot comes with its own set of challenges. We have no sooner found the ideal setting than a sudden change in weather forces us to seek alternatives. Little I knew that scouting isn't just about beautiful landscapes; it's about logistics, permissions, and navigating unpredictable elements. When only all the pieces fall into place does the magic of filmmaking truly begin to unfold.

FRONTING

4 Match the sentences 1–6 with the type of fronting a–f.

1 From my window I can see the temple.
2 So peaceful is this island that I want to live here!
3 Worse than a delayed flight is the stress of dealing with lost luggage.
4 A: I'm taking this room.
   B: Taking it, are you?
5 In the end, we asked someone for directions.
6 Most rewarding was the shower at the end of the long trek.

a adverbial phrases of time
b adverbial phrases of place
c *so* + adjective + *that*
d comparative phrases
e superlative adjectives
f a question form to respond with surprise / disagreement

5 Put the words in the correct order.

1 for Least was the me boat enjoyable trip.
2 this city that So we'll huge need is weeks!
3 trek than be would a river Easier walk a.
4 you'll bag find a in fan my.
5 A: I'm dying from this heat.
   B: you are Dying,?
6 space In the could future be the norm travel.

6 Rewrite the sentences using fronting structures.

1 We learnt all about the history of the museum before we visited.
2 We had a lovely picnic by that lake.
3 The trip was so fun that I want to go back again next month!
4 Exploring a new city by bike is better than walking.
5 The city was full of tourists. It was busiest in the summer.
6 A: That's my seat.
   B: Is it your seat,?

7 >>> STRETCH! Correct ten mistakes with inversion and fronting structures in the underlined sections.

Last week our school visited a historical palace, and honestly, ¹never I have enjoyed a school trip so much! ²So captivating the guide that I went home wanting to read loads more about its history, and that really isn't my thing at all! I think that ³more educational any classroom lecture is getting to experience something. ⁴Not were we only exploring the castle's secret passages, but also reading the diaries of the people that lived there. ⁵Rarely I never learnt so much about history! ⁶It was at the end of the day the highlight of the trip – the reenactment of a historic battle with actors and horses. We went up to the tower to watch that, and ⁷such awe-inspiring was the view from there that we took loads of selfies! ⁸It was less enjoyable, however, was the long bus ride back, which took four hours. ⁹Most disappointing part was when we got close to the town, we joined a huge traffic jam. School trips are never perfect, ¹⁰they aren't really!

8 Write about a school trip that you enjoyed. Use fronting and inversion structures.

VOCABULARY

TRAVEL IDIOMS

1 Complete the travel idioms. Use the letters to help you.

1 Don't worry, let's cross that b_____ when we come to it, we still have time.
2 Can we go back to the hostel for a nap? I've just completely run out of s_____!
3 On second thoughts, I'd prefer a beach holiday. Would you mind doing a U-t_____?
4 I love it here. Later down the l_____ I'd like to live here.
5 Let get back on t_____ and make a decision on a hotel.
6 I've done this trek before; it'll be plain s_____.
7 I just booked a round-the-world trip and I'm f_____ high with excitement!
8 I've been back for a month but I've already got i_____-feet!

2 Rewrite the sentences using idioms from Exercise 1.

1 We explored the city all morning, but by afternoon, we were completely exhausted.
2 Once we sorted out the initial confusion with our booking, the rest of the trip went smoothly.
3 I'm not sure what to do if our flight gets cancelled, but we'll deal with it when we need to.
4 When the weather turned bad, we decided to make a drastic change, and planned some indoor activities.
5 Every few months, I start dreaming of different places to go and start planning my next travel adventure.
6 After winning a free vacation in a competition, I was over the moon for days.
7 A few years in the future, I'd love to return to this island for another holiday.
8 After a few travel delays, we finally returned to the schedule and arrived at our holiday destination.

UNIT 9 TRAVEL BUG | 79

LISTENING

1 🔊 **9.1 Listen to part of a podcast on how to save money on train travel. Which tips are mentioned?**

1. Book far in advance
2. Set up fare alerts
3. Use student discounts
4. Look for last-minute deals
5. Buy a return ticket

2 Use the words in the box to complete the text.

> change expect fillers lost
> mean over similar unlike

What to ¹_____ when listening to conversations between groups of friends

1 Irregular structure: ²_____ scripted speech, conversations jump between topics and sometimes ³_____ direction. When making notes, draw arrows to a new area to help you remember it was a change.

2 ⁴_____ and pauses: It's natural to say things like *um*, *oh* or *I* ⁵_____ when talking to friends. Being aware of this can help you.

3 Multiple voices: In a conversation of more than two people, it's easy to get ⁶_____ especially if they have ⁷_____-sounding voices. When you want to listen carefully for one specific person, it can help to draw columns for each person talking and make notes in those.

4 Overlapping speech: Sometimes when people get excited, they talk ⁸_____ each other, making it difficult to hear what was said. Try to pick out key words, as that's what the speakers will be doing.

3 Which of the above were features of the podcast segment you heard? Did any of them cause you difficulties?

4 🔊 **9.1 Listen again and make notes. Use the tips above to help you track the conversation.**

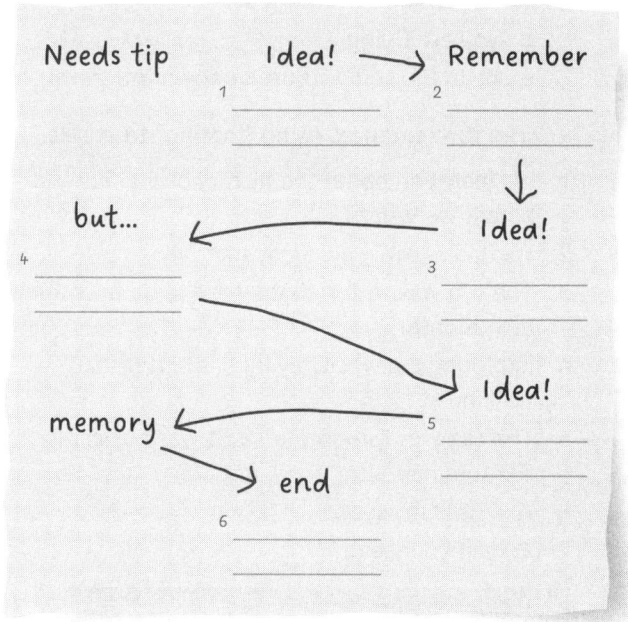

5 💼 **Innovation and Problem Solving** What tips would you give Sara about cheap train travel? Write a short message explaining your ideas.

WRITING

A FORMAL EMAIL/LETTER

1 Tick the three situations in which someone is most likely to need to write a formal email or letter.

1. For a character reference
2. For a postcard
3. For a university/college application
4. For a volunteering position application
5. For catching up with a friend

2 Complete the formal phrases with the words from the box. In which situation from Exercise 1 would you use these phrases?

> candidate   hesitate   need
> reason   response   role

1 My _____ for writing is to …
2 I am writing in _____ to a request for …
3 I feel confident that he/she would perform well in the _____ because …
4 I consider him/her to be a suitable _____ because …
5 Please do not _____ to contact me with further questions.
6 I am available to give further information should you _____ it.

EXAM TIP

Letters and emails don't only need to tell a story, they need to carry out a function, e.g. reassure somebody, justify something or persuade someone. When reading the exam task, try to identify what the function is.

3 Communication Read the exam task. What is the function of the letter? Which of the extracts below perform that function well? Why? Why are the others not suitable?

1 She's studied Physics at university, so I'm sure she's not too bad at doing research.
2 He is highly motivated to expand his knowledge in the field of education and he is dedicated to learning new skills.
3 When I tutored her on the course, she was the only student to successfully create a team management system, showing she has a unique drive.
4 He's quite good at managing people. He volunteered at a summer camp, so he had to do it there, he could do it again in this role.

4 Read the task below and plan your formal letter. Make notes for each paragraph.

1	Introduction	
2	Paragraph 1 (give evidence)	
3	Paragraph 2 (give evidence)	
4	Conclusion (summarise suitability)	

EXAM TASK WRITING PART 2

You have received a letter from James Walker, the manager of a travel agency, asking you to write a character reference for your friend Alex, who has applied for a job as a tour guide in your town.

> … Please could you include information in your letter about how you know the applicant and why this person is suited for the job of tour guide. The position consists of showing groups of visitors the main sights and giving them interesting information about the town. The successful applicant will need good communication skills and a welcoming personality ….

5 Write your letter in reply in 220–260 words. You do not need to include postal addresses.

SELF-EVALUATION

Check your writing:

Content: Do you answer both main questions asked? Have you carried out the function the task asks for?

Communication: Are your recommendations clear to the reader?

Organisation: Is the text well-organised and linked? Is there a good flow of ideas?

Language: Have you used a variety of structures and vocabulary? Have you included some new language from this unit?

HOLDING A FISHBOWL DISCUSSION

1 SETTING UP

The question we'll discuss is:
_____

I'm working with:
_____

My main arguments are:
_____
_____
_____
_____

Some opposing views could be:
_____
_____
_____
_____

2 USING A RANGE OF LINGUISTIC DEVICES

Inversion:

Fronting:

My engaging sentences with …

Reported speech:

Anything else?

Conditionals:

TIP Make sure you get a turn in big group discussions by knowing how to interrupt politely.

Some ways to interrupt politely are:
_____
_____
_____

3 EXPRESSING OPINIONS WITH SUPPORTING REASONS

It's a good idea to have supporting reasons for an opinion because …
_____
_____

Have all these opinions got supporting reasons?

What short phrases can you use to signal that you have another point to make?
_____
_____

ORACY 5

Collaboration and Teamwork

4 RESPECTING AND BUILDING ON THE VIEWS OF OTHERS

Ways you can respect others in a discussion:
___

Reasons it's good to build on what others say:
___

Phrases you can use to build on what others say:
___

Questions you can ask others to help them build on what you say:
___

After the discussion:
I talked to classmate _____ about what he/she contributed, and she/he gave me feedback. I need to think more about …
___

CHECKLIST

	Me	My partner
I've decided with my classmate _____ that we'll give each other feedback.		
After the discussion: 3, 2, 1: 3 interesting things that were mentioned		
2 adjectives to describe how I feel now I feel …		
1 point I made really well		

SELF-EVALUATION

I can …
- use a range of linguistic devices. ○
- give reasons to support my opinions. ○
- respect and build on the views of others. ○

UNIT 9 TRAVEL BUG

REVIEW 3 UNITS 7–9

GRAMMAR 1

1 Choose the correct options to complete the text.

In the past, no-one imagined that we ¹ *won't / wouldn't* only use a watch for keeping time. The first digital watches appeared in the early 70s, but people thought these ² *were / were going to be* a total flop, due to their cost of over €2,000. But they were a success, and some even imagined they ³ *were going to make / were making* analogue watches obsolete, which of course they didn't. What people didn't expect was that digital watches ⁴ *would / were going to* evolve, and in a big way. Smartwatches taking calls and texts now dominate the market. No-one could have guessed watches ⁵ *will / would* be miniature computers by the 2010s. At that time, people also ⁶ *don't / didn't* even expect we would have computers that could fit in our hands. Where were watches ⁷ *going to go / going* from there? No-one would guess. Could the 70s digital watch designers have imagined a future where watches ⁸ *would / wouldn't* track their steps, and monitor heart rates? No way. A watch as a health accessory was unimaginable for that generation!

2 Complete the conversation with the correct form of the verb in brackets.

Pilar: This time next week you ¹ _____ (sit) in a lecture room. You ² _____ (become) an undergraduate student, officially! Are you excited?

Adel: Yes and no. I'm nervous too. This time next week I ³ _____ (meet) new people every day. I'm quite introverted, so I know I'll be exhausted.

Pilar: You'll be fine. By Sunday night you ⁴ _____ (meet) your flatmates, so that's one less group to worry about.

Adel: I know. I wonder if any of them ⁵ _____ (study) for an environmental engineering degree too.

Pilar: I'm sure they ⁶ _____ (do) something similar at least. The university housing department usually puts people doing similar courses together.

Adel: Well, I ⁷ _____ (find out) soon, I guess. I'd better finish packing!

Pilar: You'd better! At nine o'clock tomorrow exactly we ⁸ _____ (get) in the car. I want to beat the traffic!

VOCABULARY 1

1 Choose the correct options to complete the conversation.

Jakob: That new mobile looks amazing. It says it's unavailable ¹ *to / for* buy in this country just now, but is coming out in a few months.

Ali: I know. They say the camera is ² *comparing / comparable* to a professional one.

Jakob: It's so cool, but my mum thinks it's inappropriate ³ *for / of* me to spend so much money on something I might just lose or break.

Ali: My brother says that too, but they're not the most knowledgeable people ⁴ *by / about* tech stuff, are they? They just use it for chatting. I mean, if someone is ⁵ *dedicated / dedicating* to making professional videos, they need a good camera. Mine is OK, but I want to work in tech, so I don't want to be ⁶ *advantaged / disadvantaged* by having an average camera.

Jakob: I know, and my family is ⁷ *supportive / unsupportive* of me wanting to be a streamer in most respects. It's just the money that's the issue.

Ali: Would it be acceptable ⁸ *with / to* borrow some money, and pay it back from the money we'll make from streaming?

Jakob: Hey, you might have a good idea there …

2 Find and correct seven errors with idioms in the article.

More and more people are buying electric vehicles and home appliances with improved energy efficiency. Taken in face value, this seems like we're tackling the climate crisis well. However, research says that change by individuals isn't enough to meet world goals for lowering CO_2 levels. In the nutshell, huge changes by multinational companies are also required. Yet transitioning from fossil fuels is easier said than made for businesses. It isn't that these companies are closing a blind eye to these issues, which we know from the 20th century can go hand with hand with disaster. What the issue may be now is a lack of green technological research. Funding green projects is an opportunity to get the best of all worlds – cleaner environment and technological advancements. Let's do the record straight, we're doing well, but we need science to help us now.

GRAMMAR 2

1 Choose the correct options to complete the text.

Have you ever looked at your dog and asked yourself why it ¹ *seems / has seemed* so happy? I investigated this for my undergraduate dissertation. As expected, research said lots of exercise and a good diet ² *had been found / found* to boost serotonin levels, but I also found two other facts ³ *being / to be* extremely interesting. One was that animals naturally engage in play, which contributes to their happiness levels. Researchers claimed that this ⁴ *was / has been* equally important for humans. They ⁵ *added / added to* that this meant humans making more time for hobbies if they wanted to be happier.

I also read an article that ⁶ *revealed / promised* that socialising made some pack animals, like dogs, happy. However, they also ⁷ *agreed / pointed out* that animals and humans had a natural limit to the size of their social circles. Studies considered the average person ⁸ *to / would* be capable of maintaining around 150 relationships, far fewer than the virtual connections we have now. They strongly advised that people ⁹ *---- / must* focus on those friends who truly matter. I think we can all ¹⁰ *agree / remind* that we have something to learn from animals when it comes to happiness.

2 Find and correct seven errors in the text.

A few years ago, my friend Sirin told that she was considering going to the shelter to adopt a cat. That time was a difficult phase in her life. She admitted to feel lost and unmotivated after leaving university. I recommended to give it a try, thinking it might bring some companionship into her life.

When Pamuk the cat came home with her, everything changed. I mean, it was expecting that life would change a little, but hers changed a lot! After a week Sirin was happier, smiley and getting up early to take her cat for a walk! It is saying that pets can provide emotional support, but seeing the way Pamuk transformed Sirin's daily routine was remarkable. Did you know it's estimates that people with pets walk thousands of extra steps a year? It's true.

Looking back, Sirin said she felt Pamuk's adoption being the best decision she had ever made. She even persuaded me to getting a cat!

VOCABULARY 2

1 Choose the correct word from the box to complete the conversation. There are two extra words.

> decommissioned hypercritical midweek
> nonviolent midweek overused post-war
> pre-industrial reclaimed underfunded

Ade: I feel so pessimistic about the future sometimes. It seems like every eco-friendly project is always ¹ _____ .

Lin: I know, and then people get ² _____ of them, saying progress isn't fast enough. But change takes time.

Ade: True. Did you hear about the wetlands project near here? The council has ³ _____ some land around a factory for birds. It hadn't been used at all ⁴ _____ , so needed regenerating.

Lin: Oh, I saw a post about that! They need volunteers. Are you free anytime ⁵ _____ ? We could help.

Ade: Well, that's why I'm feeling so down. The factory was ⁶ _____ decades ago, but the land is still really polluted because chemicals were ⁷ _____ for years. The birds wouldn't survive there.

Lin: Wow, that's so sad. I hope they find a new use for the land.

2 Choose the correct options to complete the conversation.

Phillipe: I feel that for our animal project, it would be good to focus on something like the polar bear.

Omar: Good choice! Silly question – they're ¹ *cold-blooded / marine*, right?

Phillipe: No, they're ² *mammals / predators*, so they're warm-blooded. I mean, their ³ *migration / natural habitat* is the ice and the arctic seas; they do live in the cold. I read an article warning us that polar bears are changing ⁴ *migration / prey* patterns. They're moving to warmer places to find food, then dying.

Omar: They're ⁵ *savage / predators* of other animals smaller than them, right? Like seals, fish, other ⁶ *marine / mammal* life?

Phillipe: Yep, they've got sharp teeth and they're ⁷ *fierce / predator* hunters – their main ⁸ *prey / natural habitat* is seals. They hunt them from the ice. It's so sad that ⁹ *in their natural habitat / in captivity* they just have fish thrown at them.

REVIEW 3 | 85

REVIEW 3 UNITS 7–9

GRAMMAR 3

1 Choose the correct options to complete the text.

¹ *Never / Always* did I imagine that being a tour guide would give me the opportunity to practise so many languages. Not only ² *do I / I* get to meet people from all over the world, ³ *but / than* I also immerse myself in different cultures daily. ⁴ *Rarely / Little* do I finish a tour without speaking at least three languages in a single day, which I love. Only after ⁵ *did I become / I became* a tour guide did I realise how quickly I could improve my language skills. ⁶ *Not often / No sooner* does a day pass when I don't discover a new word or phrase from chatting with a visitor. ⁷ *Only when / Little* did I know that this role would help me refine my fluency in such a natural and enjoyable way. Honestly, I highly recommend it as a summer job. Nowhere else ⁸ *have I felt / I have felt* such a sense of fulfilment, combining my love for languages with the joy of showing people new places.

2 Rewrite the text with fronting structures. Use the underlined phrases to help you.

Need to learn a language fast? My language exchange in Colombia was <u>so good</u> that I'm writing to tell everyone all about it. I spent two fantastic weeks doing a Spanish language exchange <u>there</u>. I hugged my host family goodbye <u>on the last day</u>, and this is the selfie we took together. The San Felipe castle can be seen <u>in the background of the photo</u>, where I had my second favourite day in Cartagena. The birthday party that my host family threw for me was <u>the best day I had there</u>! I really got on well with them and they helped me so much with Spanish. Chatting with them was <u>better than any Spanish class</u>. Saying goodbye was <u>the worst part of my trip</u> ☹ I hope we stay in touch!

SELF-ASSESSMENT!

3 Look back at your work in Units 7–9.

- ☐ plans and predictions in the past
- ☐ future continuous and future perfect
- ☐ reported speech – structures with *that*
- ☐ reported speech – structures without *that*
- ☐ inversion
- ☐ fronting

1 Tick ✓ the area of grammar that you feel most confident about.
2 Circle the area of grammar that you need to work on more.
3 Underline the area of grammar that you think you will use most in future.

VOCABULARY 3

1 Find and correct eight errors with travel collocations and phrases in the conversation.

Gaia: I need a holiday! Could we get away from it but still be eco-friendly? I don't want to go on a holiday package either.

Ivan: I think so. Once you start looking, there are loads of places offering more than everything-inclusive resorts. Iceland is one.

Gaia: Wow, I'd love to do the sightseeing there … the glaciers, the northern lights, sounds amazing. Let's start researching!

Ivan: OK, so good news first. There are loads of catered flights there. And, I found an amazing own-catering cottage near a volcano. Or one near the beach that offers half meals and has its own organic farm.

Gaia: And the bad news?

Ivan: Even in spring, it could bevery cold.

Gaia: I don't care, I think it'll be the holiday lifetime. Let's book it!

2 Choose the correct idioms to complete the text.

Holidays are about ¹ *getting itchy feet / flying high*, deciding to go away, then relaxing. Right? Maybe not. One survey in the USA reported that the majority of adults experience high stress levels related to holidays. One stress trigger is planning. It's easy to ² *be plain sailing / run out of steam* before the trip even starts. Keep in mind that all this hard work will mean that further ³ *down the line / back on track* you can relax. Then there is the journey there. Unexpected bad weather or potential delays can make it seem anything but ⁴ *plain sailing / doing a U-turn*. When things seem like they could go wrong, remind yourself to ⁵ *cross that bridge when you come to it / do a U-turn*.

SELF-ASSESSMENT!

3 Look back at your work in Units 7–9.

- ☐ adjectives with dependent prepositions
- ☐ idioms
- ☐ adjectives with prefixes
- ☐ the animal kingdom
- ☐ travel collocations and phrases
- ☐ travel idioms

1 Tick ✓ the vocabulary group that had the most new words for you.
2 Circle the vocabulary group that you need to work on more.
3 Underline the vocabulary group that you think you will use most in future.

VOCABULARY REFERENCE 7-9

UNIT 7

acceptable to agreeable or satisfactory to someone
comparable to similar in size, amount, or quality to something else
dedicated to having a strong commitment to a task
disadvantaged by in worse conditions than others
hostile to showing strong dislike
inappropriate for not suitable
inferior to lower in quality, or importance
isolated by separated from others, alone
knowledgeable about having a lot of knowledge
superior to better than others in quality, or importance
supportive of providing help or encouragement to someone or something
unavailable to not accessible
a pain in the neck very annoying
easier said than done a good idea in theory but hard to achieve/realise
face the music accept consequences or criticism
go hand in hand (with) be closely related
in a nutshell very briefly, to summarise
set the record straight give the correct information about something that has been misunderstood
take (something) at face value believe something without thinking about it very much
the best of both worlds the advantages of two different situations
turn a blind eye to (something) choose to ignore something bad

UNIT 8

antinuclear against nuclear power or weapons
decommissioned taken out of use, especially after being in service
hypercritical excessively critical, often to an unreasonable degree
midweek occurring in the middle of the week
nonviolent not using violence
overused used too much
postwar happening or existing after a war, typically referring to the period after World War II
pre-industrial before the industrial era or revolution
reclaimed taken back or recovered
semi-permanent lasting for a limited period of time, not fully permanent
ultra-expensive extremely expensive, more than usually expected
underfunded not receiving enough financial support or resources to function properly
cold/warm-blooded relating to body temperature of a living thing
fierce violent or aggressive
in captivity not allowed to live in the wild
mammal an animal that feeds milk to its young
marine relating to the sea
migration moving from one region to another
natural habitat the environment in which a species usually lives
predator an animal that hunts and eats other animals
prey an animal that is eaten by another animal
savage extremely violent

UNIT 9

all-inclusive resort a place for holidays with a fixed price for all accommodation, food, and entertainment
break the journey stop and rest on the way from one place to another
charter flight flight on an airplane rented by a travel company or other organisation
come to a standstill stop moving or working
do the sights see all the places typically visited
full board hotel accommodation including breakfast, lunch, and dinner
get away from it all go away and forget about your problems or responsibilities
half board hotel accommodation including breakfast and lunch or dinner
holiday of a lifetime the best holiday
package holiday an organised holiday with a fixed price for accommodation, food, and usually travel
scheduled flight a regular flight organised by the airline itself
self-catering accommodation a holiday house or flat where you cook for yourself
back on track going as planned again, after a problem
(be) plain sailing happen easily, with no problems
cross that bridge when you come to it don't worry about future problems, solve them if they really happen
do a U-turn completely change your opinion or plans
down the line at a later time
flying high very happy or excited
get/have itchy feet start wanting to travel or to change something in your life
run out of steam lose motivation for something you have been doing

DIGITAL CLASSROOM
PRACTICE EXTRA UNITS 7-9

EXPLORING EMPLOYABILITY 1

INNOVATION AND PROBLEM SOLVING

1 THINK

1.1 Read the excuses 1–6. Then think of situations when these (or similar excuses) could be given to not do something.

1. I've never used this programme before.
2. These instructions are in Dutch, and I don't speak Dutch.
3. I always take my sister to school on Monday.
4. I'm a morning person.
5. The last bus is at 19.00.
6. Jan and I never work well together.

1.2 What possible solutions could you give to 1–6 in Exercise 1.1? Write your own suggestions.

1.3 Match solutions a–f to reasons 1–6 in Exercise 1.1. Then rate the responses from 1–10, according to how likely you think they are to have a positive result (1 = very unlikely, 10 = very likely).

a We can discuss the things that relate to your work before then.
b Why not see if there's a training video on YouTube?
c If you can find them online, you could put them into a translation app.
d Then use this as a chance to find a way of dealing with your differences.
e If I send you the work last thing at night, would that work?
f Could you possibly swap days with someone else?

2 ENGAGE

2.1  Watch the video. Complete the table with notes on the positive (P) and negative (N) things the colleagues say about each other.

	Cam	Reese	Ashley
Cam		P	P
		N	N
Reese	P		P
	N		N
Ashley	P	P	
	N	N	

3 EXPLORE

3.1 Imagine Cam, Reese and Ashley are in your team. Read the suggestions below. What would you do to solve their problems? Why?

1. Nothing. There are always some problems between team members. It's natural.
2. Establish a set of strict rules everyone has to follow.
3. Get everyone together and discuss the problems.
4. Make one of them a senior group member who has the power to tell the others what to do.

3.2 Look at the following ideas. Which do you think could be useful in this situation and why?

1. Look at things from other people's perspective.
2. Think outside the box.
3. Don't take sides.
4. Get someone to act as a mediator.
5. Brainstorm possible solutions as a team.

3.3 Based on your own experience of finding solutions, complete the following sentences with your own ideas.

1. When people think outside the box …
2. If you take sides in a disagreement …
3. The advantage of having a mediator is …
4. The value of brainstorming ideas as a team is …
5. Although it can be difficult to look at things from another perspective …

3.4 It's important to use effective language when suggesting and negotiating. This usually means being respectful, asking questions and proposing solutions. Look at the examples below and match the sentences 1–6 with the continuations a–f.

1. I'd like you to tell us more …
2. I'm sure there are a number of things …
3. This is an opportunity to develop a …
4. I'm certainly happy to …
5. I understand your position, but I have …
6. So can we now agree that this is …

a … the way forward?
b … about what the consequences of your decision would be.
c … we can agree on here.
d … some doubts I'd like to discuss.
e … keep an open mind and consider your suggestions.
f … collaboration that helps everyone.

4 CREATE

4.1 Read the team leader Tara's summary of the situation with Cam, Reese and Ashley to her manager. Which of the problems she mentions sounds most difficult to solve?

> I think there are a number of problems in the office at the moment. I've had an email from a customer who was annoyed because she had a problem she urgently needed Cam to solve, but he wasn't in the office so she didn't get the help she needed.
>
> I'm aware that Cam has some personal issues at home, so we've agreed that he can start between 9:30 and 10 o'clock, and then stay late. These hours work best for him.
>
> Then I spoke to Reese this morning. He says Cam's always late and arrives whenever he wants.
>
> And then Ashley was annoyed because Reese complains a lot about Cam. Her workload is another problem. When I spoke to her last month, she said she wanted more responsibility, but now I wonder if she has too much to do.
>
> So, perhaps Reese thinks he works harder than Cam, or Cam isn't serious about his job. It could be that Reese doesn't know about Cam's personal problems. Maybe Cam doesn't want everyone to know about them.
>
> I wonder how we can solve these problems. I'm going to suggest a meeting with all three colleagues. What do you think?

4.2 Look back at your ideas for Exercises 3.1, 3.2 and 3.3. Write Tara a message with suggestions on how to solve the problems in her team. Write your opinion in 250–300 words.

5 REFLECT

1. Were you able to give Tara clear, useful advice?
2. Did you include language from these pages?
3. How could you improve your message?
4. What skills do you think are needed to help solve disagreements between people?
5. The situation you explored in these pages was in a work context. What similar situations can happen among friends or at school?

EXPLORING EMPLOYABILITY 2

COLLABORATION AND TEAMWORK

 **THINK**

1.1 Make a list of different teams or groups you have been part of in the last two years. On a scale of 1–10 (1 = worst, 10 = best) rank them according to how positive the experience was. What made the experience more positive or negative?

2 ENGAGE

2.1 Look at the three photos of people working together. What kinds of skills do you think they need to collaborate effectively?

2.2 Look at some examples of what people in the pictures are thinking. Which picture (A, B or C) do 1–6 relate to? More than one answer is possible.

1 I thought we decided I was going to do that.
2 I'm going to ask her to explain how to do that because it looks very useful.
3 This is interesting, but we haven't really got a plan about what to do first.
4 Right, so let's agree on who's doing what now this part is almost finished.
5 I think it's important to tell them they did a great job here.
6 Should I remind everyone that this part must be finished by Monday?

2.3 Which examples in 2.2 suggest a group has a good working relationship? Which ones don't? Why?

3 EXPLORE

3.1  Watch a video in which three co-workers are planning to produce an information pack. Who does the following things, Sabrina, Tara or Leo?

1 Refers to a useful example of a previous project.
2 Agrees to takes responsibility for a task.
3 Congratulates someone on doing something well.
4 Points out a problem relating to time.
5 Estimates the time they need to do something.
6 Summarises what has been decided.

3.2 When we work in groups or teams we need to choose or allocate tasks. Match the tasks 1–5 to the best person for the role a–e.

1 talking to clients or customers
2 arranging transport
3 coming up with new ideas
4 checking everyone is doing their work
5 creating timetables and schedules

a I'm very good at looking at the big picture and like making sure we haven't missed anything. I keep detailed notes so people can always ask me what their priorities should be.
b I like finding the best routes, planning delivery times and telling people they can expect deliveries on time!
c I've always been creative. I love trying out things and experimenting.
d Communication is my strong point, for sure, and I'm very sociable. I think I make a positive impression.
e A lot of people find working with spreadsheets and numbers boring, but I love it – it's a bit like solving a puzzle, you know, making sure all the pieces fit together.

4 CREATE

4.1 Your school has asked you and three other students to be the welcome committee for an exchange student programme. Read the responsibilities and the information on the committee members below. Then prepare a proposed distribution of tasks for the group.

> Responsibilities of the volunteers:
> Writing a welcoming email
> Being available to help the visitors
> Arranging some welcome events
> Taking the visitors on a guided tour of the city

5 REFLECT

1. What did you take into consideration when deciding which tasks people should do?
2. Do you think you allocate people well?
3. Is there anyone who was more difficult to allocate?
4. What would you do if you saw that someone was not happy with their task?
5. Who would you talk to if you felt the group wasn't working as well as it should?

You: SHY WITH STRANGERS; GOOD AT LANGUAGES; GOOD AT PLANNING

Mara: IMAGINATIVE; NOT PUNCTUAL; SPORTY; SOCIABLE

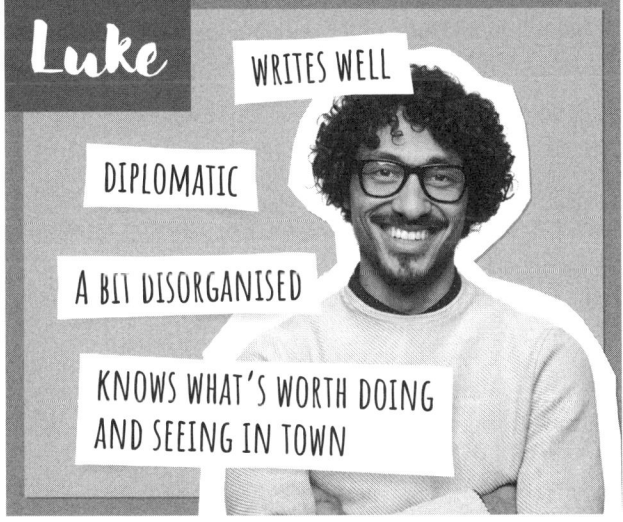

Luke: WRITES WELL; DIPLOMATIC; A BIT DISORGANISED; KNOWS WHAT'S WORTH DOING AND SEEING IN TOWN

Katy: FLEXIBLE; ALWAYS AVAILABLE AND HELPFUL; GOOD WITH SOCIAL MEDIA; GOOD AT PUBLIC SPEAKING

EXPLORING EMPLOYABILITY 3

CRITICAL THINKING AND DECISION MAKING

 THINK

1.1 Complete at the quotations with a word from the box.

> broke   creative   depends   fear   perspective

1. If it ain't _____, don't fix it. (Bert Lance)

2. Everyone has a time _____ – we are past, present or future focused, in a positive or negative way. (Philip Zimbardo)

3. The future _____ on what you do today. (Mahatma Gandhi)

4. We did not come to _____ the future. We came here to shape it. (Obama)

5. The future belongs to those who learn more skills and combine them in _____ ways. (Robert Greene)

1.2 What do the quotations have in common? Which quotation is the most interesting? Which do you agree or disagree with?

ENGAGE

2.1 Match the reasons why people might not want to change a system or process 1–5 to the responses a–e.

1. I get very anxious when I have to change how I do something.
2. The system I use at the moment works perfectly well.
3. It's risky trying something that requires new skills.
4. Even if this system is better, it means spending more money.
5. I don't want to waste my time learning a new way of doing something.

a. True, but it might not be suitable for the new format.
b. Look, it might actually save you time in the long run.
c. On the other hand, you might enjoy getting out of your comfort zone.
d. You should see that as an investment, not an expense.
e. Your team are very supportive so you can always ask them for help.

2.2 Critical thinking often means challenging and testing your ideas by asking yourself questions. Read comments a–d below. Do you agree with them? Now look at responses a–e in Exercise 2.1 again. Would any of them make you change your mind?

a. There are cheaper versions of this, so why spend so much on this one?
b. I've never done anything like this. I'm afraid I'll be a disaster.
c. I've been doing it this way for years and nobody has ever complained.
d. This means giving up my free time, and why should I?

2.3 ▶ Watch the video. Frank, Donna and Justin are talking about changing their company contracts from paper to electronic format. Which pros and cons do they mention?

3 EXPLORE

3.1 Watch the video again. Are the statements true, false or is the information not given?

1. There is no hurry to make a decision about electronic contracts.
2. The meeting is conducted in a respectful way.
3. Irrelevant topics are mentioned in the discussion.
4. Everyone listens to each other's ideas.
5. Everyone assumes Frank will take the decision.
6. The company will probably benefit from moving to electronic contracts.

4 CREATE

4.1 In some situations, it is useful or necessary to present ideas in a formal, structured way. Look at the skills in the box. When writing, which of these do you feel you do well and which would you like to improve?

- ☐ Analysing information
- ☐ Interpreting data
- ☐ Evaluating arguments and proposals
- ☐ Reaching conclusions
- ☐ Collecting and organising relevant information
- ☐ Evaluating options and recommendations
- ☐ Justifying decisions

4.2 You recently attended a meeting to discuss how an empty classroom in your school could be used. The school has asked you to write a proposal giving your assessment of three possible options. Read the notes you took below.

4.3 Using your notes, and referencing the skills in 4.1, plan the structure of your proposal. Then write your proposal in 250–300 words.

5 REFLECT

1. How did you feel about writing your proposal?
2. Would you expect to receive a positive response? Why? / Why not?
3. Have you included all the skills in 4.1?
4. What would you say are your strengths as a critical thinker and decision maker? Are there any specific aspects you would like to improve in?

Present: Ana, David, Fernanda, Marcus

Proposal: A quiet / self-study room

> **A** pointed out that the multi-media centre already offers this. **D** said most people put up with noise and don't need this kind of space. **F** didn't feel strongly about this one way or another. **M** has doubts about people using it outside exam times.

Proposal: A space school clubs can book for events

> **A** suggested this would be a positive addition. Clubs don't have a dedicated space. **D** said it might lead to some problems – double bookings, keeping it tidy – who is responsible for that? **F** wondered if the clubs could be allocated specific times to avoid any disagreements. **M** made the point that this means the room would only be used by club members. What about everyone else?

Proposal: A fund-raising shop (second-hand games, bake sale, etc.)

> **A** thought it's a great idea, but potentially complicated to run and organize. **D** claimed it could be a really good opportunity to learn about organising and planning. **F** proposed the student council to run this – also important to discuss how money is managed. **M** put forward the idea this could be a different fund-raiser each month, sometimes for the school and other times for charity.

EXPLORING EMPLOYABILITY 4

LEADERSHIP AND GLOBAL CITIZENSHIP

1.1 Look at the statements about experiences of being a leader, or about leaders people have worked with. Do they remind you of situations you have experienced? Why? / Why not?

1. I had such a great team that I actually didn't have to do much except check everyone was ready.

2. Most of the time I didn't get the support and advice I needed to make a useful contribution.

3. I insisted that if anyone had a problem, or felt they were not getting the help they needed, we should talk about it immediately.

4. From the start, it was obvious we were expected to do what we were told and not ask questions.

5. I realised that I'm much happier having someone direct me than being the one in charge.

6. I would have preferred someone more direct – strict even – I didn't know what I was supposed to do half the time.

7. At first, I wasn't really motivated, but once she explained the importance of what we were doing, I became totally involved.

2.1 Look at the photos of teams and groups. How would you describe the role and responsibilities of the leader in these situations?

2.2 Which leadership qualities do you think are most important? Rank the qualities from 1–5 (1 = most important, 5 = least important).

a The ability to explain and define objectives
b The ability to motivate and inspire people
c Having a clear understanding of individual
d Knowing your strengths and weaknesses
e Having patience and empathy
f Paying attention to details

3 EXPLORE

3.1 Read the email below. How convincing is it? How likely are you to get involved?

> Inbox   4 Messages
>
> Hi,
>
> How are you? I know it's been a while since we spoke, so I'm excited to tell you about an initiative I'm now involved in that – knowing your interest in environmental and social issues – could really interest you.
>
> We recently created a 'Walkability' project here in Caltown. Did you know you can go to a website, type in your address, and it will tell you how 'walkable' your town, city or neighbourhood is? Really! I mean, have you ever asked yourself whether it is possible to walk to school, the shops, the sports centre and other places you go to? And what about your parents, can they walk to work? Are there some parts of the town it's hard to walk to because it means crossing busy, even dangerous roads? And what about opportunities for walking – have you got parks and gardens near where you live? Are there safe, clean paths people can use for exercise and to get fresh air?
>
> Personally, I think it's a great initiative! We would all benefit from walking more and this makes it so easy!
>
> I've attached a couple of links for you to have a look at. I know you're great at getting things done, so how about taking the lead in your town to make people aware of how important 'walkability' is?
>
> Apart from that, what's the latest news about …

4 CREATE

4.1 You want to form a team to promote walkability in your town. As the team leader, you decide to create a leaflet to make people aware of and join your cause. After following the links your friend sent, you have made notes on other important aspects of walkability. In addition to the ideas in your friend's message, decide which other information to include in your leaflet. Look back at the qualities identified in 2.2 and decide which ones you need to create the leaflet.

- Reduces pollution through emissions
- More contact with other people
- Saves money on transport
- Encourages use of local shops and stores
- Benefits the environment (plants and trees)
- Health benefits (for all ages)
- Makes places more attractive to visitors

4.2 Write your leaflet. Use between 250–300 words.

5 REFLECT

1. How do you think people you know would respond to your leaflet?
2. Which of the points you included do you feel would have most impact for people in your community?
3. How convincing do you think your leaflet is?
4. Do you feel it demonstrates effective leadership?
5. Are there any things you could change to make it more convincing?

VOCABULARY BUILDER

UNIT 1 MY VOCABULARY

Can you remember the vocabulary from Unit 1? Use the letters and the number of letters to help you.

LEISURE, ART AND ENTERTAINMENT

1 a _ _   e _ _ _ _ _ _ _ _ _ (3,10)
2 f _ _ _ _ _   g _ _ _ _ _ _ _ _ (6,9)
3 f _ _ _ _ _   v _ _ _ _ (6,5)
4 k _ _ _   p _ _ _ _ _ _ _ _ _ _ (4,11)
5 h _ _ _ _ _ _ _ _   c _ _ _ _ _ (9,6)
6 p _ _ _ _ _ _   v _ _ _ _ (7,5)
7 q _ _ _ _ _ _   t _ _ _ (7,4)
8 s _ _ _ _ _   w _ _ _ _ (6,5)
9 t _ _ _ _   f _ _ _ (5,4)
10 u _ _ _ _ _ _ _ _ _ _ _ _   e _ _ _ _ _ _ _ _ _ (13,10)

ARTS ADJECTIVES

11 g _ _ _ _ _ _ _ _ _ _ _ _ _ (14)
12 t _ _ _ _ _ _ (7)
13 m _ _ _ _ _ (6)
14 h _ _ _ _ _ _ _ _ (9)
15 h _ _ _ _ _ _ _ _ (9)
16 d _ _ _ _ _ _ _ _ _ (10)
17 u _ _ _ _ _ _ _ _ _ _ _ (12)
18 o _ _ _ _ _ _ _ _ (9)
19 g _ _ _ _ _ _ (7)
20 f _ _ _-f _ _ _ _ (3,7)

VOCABULARY EXTENSION

1 Read the text. Replace the underlined words or phrases with the correct option from the box.

> accomplished   fall flat   first-rate
> innovative   renowned   seriously dull
> staggering   the attendance

2 Complete the sentences with the words and phrases from Exercise 1.

1 That film was _____, I almost fell asleep.
2 The world tour was a huge success. The number of participants was _____.
3 Becoming a(n) _____ pianist requires a lot of commitment.
4 Humour doesn't translate well. Jokes can _____ in one country and not in another.
5 Their first album sold very well, they are on their way to become very _____ all over the world.
6 Due to bad weather _____ was smaller than expected.
7 The artist's work is _____. I had never seen anything like that before.
8 It was only a local play, but the acting was _____.

3 Complete the text with vocabulary from this page.

With the excuse that my older sister was making a ¹_____ visit, we decided that as well as the usual ²_____ gathering for dinner, we could do something special. That weekend in town there was a play we could see, but I had heard it was ³_____ dull and tickets were expensive. I liked the idea of seeing a new movie at the cinema – a ⁴_____ comedy according to the reviews, but a disaster if the jokes fell ⁵_____. But by chance, one of my sister's favourite bands was playing an outdoor concert – the old gardens in the city centre are the ⁶_____ venue for a warm evening. So that's what we did, and it was an ⁷_____ experience. The atmosphere was perfect, the lighting and sound were ⁸_____-rate and the band were amazing. They're going to be really ⁹_____ one day.

➡ YOUR TURN

4 Find two more words to describe leisure activities, films, concerts, and exhibitions. Write them here, with a translation or a description of the meaning.

Our Class Exhibition

Last month my art class had our first public exhibition! I was worried it would ¹be a complete failure, but in fact it turned out to be a great success, apart from the opening. Our teacher invited a ²famous painter to attend – and his welcome speech was ³so boring! Luckily, it didn't matter.

I was told by friends that there was some really ⁴original work. Not everything was ⁵excellent, but overall the paintings on display were ⁶technically very good. What amazed us was ⁷how many people went to the exhibition. I expected mostly family and friends would go along, but an ⁸unbelievable 2,000 made the effort.

96 VOCABULARY BUILDER

UNIT 2 MY VOCABULARY

Can you remember the vocabulary from Unit 2? Use the letters and the number of letters to help you.

BOOK AND STORIES

1. a _____ a _____ (9,6)
2. b ____ e _____ (4,10)
3. c _____ s _____ (10,5)
4. c _____ r _____ (10,7)
5. g _____ r _____ (7,7)
6. u _____ d _____ (11,8)
7. a _____ someone's i _____ (6,8)
8. b ____ u_ t___ s_____ (5,2,3,8)
9. h ___ someone's a _____ (4,9)
10. f ____ someone's i _____ (4,11)
11. p ____ h _____ i _ something (4,5,2)
12. w ____ t _____ something (4,7)

ADJECTIVES WITH SUFFIXES

13. a _____ (7)
14. b _____ (7)
15. h _____ (6)
16. f _____ (8)
17. i _____ (10)
18. f _____ (10)
19. i _____ (11)
20. l _____ (7)
21. p _____ (9)
22. s _____ (10)

VOCABULARY EXTENSION

1 Complete the texts with words or expressions from the boxes.

> caught on   in demand   predictable plot
> read up on   take to

📖 *Hometown* by Richard Heller

I read the first two novels in the *Hometown* series and loved them. The third one was published last month. I had to order it in advance – it was really ¹_____. The series has definitely ²_____, now it seems everyone's reading it. Overall, to be honest, it was disappointing – it's got a ³_____, and I really didn't ⁴_____ the new character who joins the group of friends – he doesn't feel real. There was also a lot of stuff about archaeology which I had to ⁵_____. I didn't know who they were talking about half the time!

> comes to   highly convincing   mixed reviews
> monotonous   raises the tension

Deep Water by Anne Gable

Deep Water is about a girl whose dream is to be an Olympic athlete, although she doesn't have many opportunities living in a little village in the mountains. I get why it had ⁶_____. On the one hand, her feelings and frustration are ⁷_____, but some of the race scenes are a bit ⁸_____. But as the story develops, Gable ⁹_____ and by the end, I was hooked. When it ¹⁰_____ showing how someone fights to achieve their dream, it's brilliant.

2 Complete the video game review with words from this page.

WildLands has to be one of the games of the year. It might also have the most ¹_____ stories of any game I've played. The makers worked with ²_____ author Max Barling, who makes no secret of his passion for the heroic *WildLands* characters. Max takes them on a lengthy and dangerous journey, ³_____ the tension with each adventure. Some people might pick ⁴_____ in the speed of the game – some sections are lengthy and frustrating. But that's just part of the game's ⁵_____ experiment with storytelling. Personally, it ⁶_____ my attention from start to finish – I got so interested in the location I ⁷_____ the history of the Caribbean as a result. When it comes to drama and surprises, there's nothing better than *WildLands*. Great game stories have really ⁸_____ on in recent years and this is a brilliant example of that trend.

➡ YOUR TURN

3 Find two more new words related to books, stories or video games. Write them here, with a translation or a description of the meaning.

UNIT 3 MY VOCABULARY

Can you remember the vocabulary from Unit 3? Use the letters and the number of letters to help you..

PERSONAL FINANCE

1 b_____ h_____ (6,7)
2 g__ i_____ d____ (3,4,4)
3 s_____ _ f_____ (5,1,7)
4 w_____ c____ (8,4)
5 c_____ p_____ (11,7)
6 c_____ a_____ (7,7)
7 d_____ d____ (6,5)
8 e_____ t_____ (10,8)
9 l___ s_____ (4,7)
10 s_____ o_ i_____ (6,2,6)
11 s_____ m_____ (5,6)
12 s_____ a__ s_____ (6,3,6)

FINANCE PHRASAL VERBS

13 b___ s_____ o__ (4,7,3)
14 d__ i___ s_____ (3,4,7)
15 c___ i__ m____ (4,4,5)
16 p__ i___ _ p_____ (3,4,1,7)
17 p__ d____ _ d_____ (3,4,1,7)
18 r____ o__ p_____ (4,3,8)
19 r__ someone o__ (3,3)
20 m____ r___ l_ (5,4,2)
21 r__ t_____ m_____ (3,7,5)
22 w___ o__ d____ (4,3,4)

VOCABULARY EXTENSION

1 Read the conversation between James (J) and Sofia (S), a financial advisor. Match the underlined words or phrases in the text to the definitions 1–5.

J: So, Sofia, will you study all the options, then advise me on me what to do?
S: That's a bit <u>behind the times</u> these days! It's mostly computer programmes which do that now.
J: Yes, but will they find me the best <u>interest rates</u>?
S: I can guarantee their <u>reliability</u>, yes.
J: I really want to make an investment in green technology.
S: OK, but you could make <u>substantially</u> more with some other companies. You might only <u>break even</u> – there could be no profit at all.
J: Well, that's a risk I'm willing to take.
S: It's your decision, I'm only pointing out the <u>drawbacks</u>.
J: Thanks, could you also advise me on taking out an insurance <u>policy</u>?
Sofia: I have a colleague who can do that. As a student, you might be entitled to a <u>subsidy</u>.
J: That would be great – I was looking at some prices to insure my flat and musical instruments and they were really <u>steep</u>! I was shocked.
S: I know, but hopefully my colleague will find you <u>a good deal</u>.

1 the percentage of money an investor receives
2 neither make money nor lose money
3 a legal agreement
4 a reasonable price
5 a grant or gift of money to help pay for something, usually given by an organization or government

2 Find underlined words or phrases in Exercise 1 that mean the opposite of 1–5.

1 cheap
2 up to date
3 not much
4 advantages
5 something you can't trust or believe

3 Complete the text with the correct form of words from this page.

When I left home to study, my uncle helped me find somewhere to live. First, we found an agency that ¹_____ out properties to students, but flats weren't cheap. I couldn't afford to spend a ²_____ and definitely didn't want to ³_____ into my savings. We looked at lots of places – some were really ⁴_____ because of their central location – and finally got a good ⁵_____ in a nice neighbourhood. I had to ⁶_____ down a deposit and payment was by ⁷_____ debit from my bank account.
In terms of my daily budget, what made a massive difference was getting a weekend job. With that ⁸_____ of income I could pay my rent and expenses. I had to be careful but I ⁹_____ even at the end of the month, and as a result I didn't get into ¹⁰_____.

➡ YOUR TURN

4 What is your experience of saving or spending money? What advice have people given you about managing money? Find two more new words or expressions to describe your ideas. Write them here, with a translation or a description of the meaning.

UNIT 4 MY VOCABULARY

Can you remember the vocabulary from Unit 4? Use the letters and the number of letters to help you.

STUDY AND EXAMS

1 a _ _ _ _ _ _ _ y _ _ _ (8,4)
2 a _ _ _ _ _ _ _ _ _ (10)
3 d _ _ _ _ _ _ _ (8)
4 f _ _ _ _ t _ _ _ (5,4)
5 f _ _ _ _ _ (6)
6 p _ _ _ _ _ _ _ _ _ (10)
7 s _ _ _ _ _ _ _ _ _ _ (11)
8 s _ _ _ _ _ _ l _ _ _ (7,4)
9 s _ _ _ _ _ _ _ (8)
10 d _ _ _ _ _ _ _ _ _ _ _ (12)
11 t _ _ _ _ _ _ f _ _ _ (7,4)
12 u _ _ _ _ _ _ _ _ _ _ _ _ (13)

EDUCATION – VERBS AND PHRASES

13 a _ _ _ _ _ _ k _ _ _ _ _ _ _ _ (7,9)
14 a _ _ _ _ _ (6)
15 c _ _ _ _ o _ _ r _ _ _ _ _ _ _ (5,3,8)
16 c _ _ _ (4)
17 d _ _ _ o _ _ (4,3)
18 k _ _ _ _ y _ _ _ s _ _ _ _ _ _
   i _ _ _ _ _ o _ _ (4,4,7,6,3)
19 m _ _ _ _ _ i _ (5,2)
20 m _ _ _ _ _ _ _ (8)
21 s _ _ _ _ _ p _ _ _ (6,1,5)
22 s _ _ _ i _ _ _ _ _ _ _ _ _ _ (4,10)
23 s _ _ _ _ _ (6)

VOCABULARY EXTENSION

1 Read the advice for new students on a university forum. Whose advice is the most useful?

ADVICE ⌄ SOCIAL ⌄ SUPPORT ⌄

GROUP WORK

You'll be doing a lot of group work on your course. This means <u>collaborating</u> with different kinds of people, so it's really important to <u>be on the same page</u> about who should do what. Some people are <u>suited to</u> creative roles while others are good at things like preparing data and graphics. Make sure work is <u>allocated</u> fairly by making a plan as a team first – that can be <u>time-consuming</u>, but will make a significant difference in the end. (Annie)

ADVICE ⌄ SOCIAL ⌄ SUPPORT ⌄

ESSAY WRITING

You might have great ideas for your essay or paper, but if you don't <u>fulfil the requirements</u>, you'll lose marks. Check things like length and how you <u>reference</u> your sources. You'll <u>grasp the basics</u> very quickly, but some things take longer – like the way you <u>evaluate</u> theories and opinions you don't agree with. It's important to show you have the <u>capacity</u> to back up your ideas. (Pedro)

2 Match the underlined words and phrases from the texts to the synonyms 1–10.

1 ability
2 agree
3 distributed
4 do what's expected
5 have the right skills for something
6 learn the essential things
7 assess
8 give sources
9 slow
10 working together

3 Complete another text from the forum with the correct options.

ADVICE ⌄ SOCIAL ⌄ SUPPORT ⌄

While preparing for the [1] *scholarly / study / academic* year you will have many important decisions to make. Many of these relate to which courses you want to take. Make sure you check [2] *outlines / deadlines / defines* carefully – it's amazing how many people forget to [3] *submit / place / hand* in their preferences on time. Read the course information and ensure you [4] *fill / fulfil / fill in* the requirements – also look carefully at timetables – some courses are scheduled on the same days. Once you have secured a place on a course, familiarise yourself with the type of exams and obligatory activities such as [5] *land / nature / field* trips or group presentations. Not all courses are exam-based – some courses give you a lot of control over your learning. You might develop an original project in order to [6] *hand / read / show* initiative. Ask yourself if that is the right course for you. Dedicating your time to preparing might be slow and [7] *time / work / thought*-consuming, but it's an essential step on your way to [8] *assembling / arranging / acquiring* knowledge.

➡ YOUR TURN

4 What is your experience of studying and taking exams? What do you think are the main challenges for students starting new courses or going to college? Find two more new words or expressions to describe your ideas. Write them here, with a translation or a description of the meaning.

VOCABULARY BUILDER | 99

UNIT 5 MY VOCABULARY

Can you remember the vocabulary from Unit 5? Use the letters and the number of letters to help you.

PERSONALITY

1. an i _ _ _ _ _ _ _ _ (9)
2. i _ _ _ _ _ _ _ _ _ _ (11)
3. an e _ _ _ _ _ _ _ _ (9)
4. e _ _ _ _ _ _ _ _ _ _ (11)
5. c _ _ _ _ _ _ _ _ _ _ _ _ (13)
6. f _ _ _ _ _ (6)
7. i _ _ _ _ _ _ _ _ _ (10)
8. i _ _ _ _ _ _ _ _ (9)
9. i _ _ _ _ _ _ _ (8)
10. m _ _ _ _ _ _ _ _ _ (10)
11. o _ _ _ _ _ _ _ _ (9)
12. p _ _ _ _ _ (6)
13. r _ _ _ _ _ _ _ (8)
14. t _ _ _ _ _ _ _ (8)

NEGATIVE PREFIXES

15. de _ _ _ _ _ _ _ _ (10)
16. dis _ _ _ _ _ _ _ (10)
17. il _ _ _ _ _ (7)
18. im _ _ _ _ _ _ _ _ _ _ _ (13)
19. in _ _ _ _ _ _ _ (9)
20. ir _ _ _ _ _ _ _ _ (10)
21. mi _ _ _ _ (6)
22. over _ _ _ _ _ (9)
23. under _ _ _ _ _ _ _ _ (13)
24. un _ _ _ _ (6)

VOCABULARY EXTENSION

1 Complete the definitions 1–10 with the words and phrases in the box.

> blunt   dare someone to do something   disloyal
> incapable of   keep your cool   misleading
> outgoing   perfection   self-centred   talkative

1. _____ is a quality in which everything is already as well as it can be and nothing can be better.
2. Someone who says exactly what they think is _____.
3. Someone who is sociable and friendly is _____.
4. If you don't support someone you should support you are _____.
5. If you only think about yourself, you are _____.
6. If you don't panic in a difficult situation you _____.
7. Someone who likes having lots of conversations is _____.
8. When you are unable to do something, you are _____ doing it.
9. If you make someone believe something that is untrue the information you give them is _____.
10. If you _____, you try to make them act by asking them to show they are brave enough.

2 Complete the text with the right form of a word or phrase from this page.

Susan Cain, author of *The Power of Introverts in a World That Can't Stop Talking*, believes quiet people who prefer to think rather than speak, have a disadvantage in many situations. People who are ¹_____ get more attention and ²_____ tend to be more successful in interviews. Cain suggests that private and quiet people are often more ³_____ – and likely to be more ⁴_____ in the way they work. Of course, appearances can be ⁵_____ and we get to know people over time. The problem Cain says is that in job or college interviews you begin from a weaker position if you are introverted. According to Cain, some people are ⁶_____ of 'selling' themselves and attracting attention because they are not ⁷_____ by nature whereas confident people who talk a lot will quickly create a good impression. In the end, as Cain points out, introverts have as much to contribute as extroverts. If you don't agree, I ⁸_____ to tell that to these three famous examples of introverts – JK Rowling, Bill Gates and Mark Zuckerberg!

→ YOUR TURN

3 Find two more new words related to personality. Write them here, with a translation or a description of the meaning.

UNIT 6 MY VOCABULARY

Can you remember the vocabulary from Unit 6?
Use the letters and the number of letters to help you.

CELEBRATIONS

1 f _ _ _ _ _ _ _ _ _ _ (11)
2 f _ _ _ _ (5)
3 r _ _ _ _ _ (6)
4 m _ _ _ _ _ _ _ _ (9)
5 s _ _ _ _ _ _ _ _ (9)
6 t _ _ _ _ _ _ _ _ _ (10)
7 b _ _ _ _ w _ _ _ t _ _ _ _ _ _ _ _ _ (5,4,9)
8 c _ _ _ o _ a _ _ (4,2,3)
9 f _ _ _ o _ _ d _ _ _ (4,2,1,3)
10 f _ _ _ i _ _ m _ _ _ _ _ (4,2,1,5)
11 m _ _ _ a _ o _ _ _ _ _ _ _ (4,2,8)
12 o _ _ _ _ _ _ _ h _ _ _ _ _ _ (7,1,7)
13 u _ _ _ _ _ _ t _ _ _ _ _ _ _ _ _ (6,1,9)

DESCRIBING CELEBRATIONS

14 a _ _ _ _ _ _ _ _ _ _ (11)
15 c _ _ _ _ _ _ _ _ (9)
16 e _ _ _ _ _ _ _ _ _ _ (11)
17 f _ _ _ _ _ _ (7)
18 f _ _ _ _ _ _ _ _ _ (10)
19 r _ _ _ _ _ _ (7)
20 t _ _ _ _ _ _ _ (8)
21 v _ _ _ _ _ _ (7)

VOCABULARY EXTENSION

1 Read an extract from a novel in which a girl visits her grandparents during a festival. Match the underlined words and phrases in the text with the definitions 1–8.

> It had been almost ten years since Keira had spent the summer with her grandparents. The sudden appearance of big tents was a <u>reminder</u> of the growing excitement as the whole village began making preparations for the annual summer solstice festival. Four days (and four <u>sleepless</u> nights) of music, food, fun and entertainment. As far as Keira could tell, nobody really knew the <u>origins</u> of the celebrations. Some said it was related to the harvest, others thought it was originally the birthday of an important person. Her grandfather, a <u>long-time</u> member of the organising committee, thought it had begun as a summer market. Whatever the reason, it was sure to be a <u>sparkling</u> event, with bright colours, fireworks and loud music – and a <u>fair</u> selling sweets, toys and clothes. It began with the <u>opening</u> speeches on Thursday night and ended with a massive <u>clean-up</u> on Monday morning. Keira knew she would love every minute of it.

1 what happens at the beginning of something
2 what you might do after a mess has been made
3 causes you to recall something
4 the opposite of boring and sad
5 staying awake, often for a long time
6 the beginning of something
7 this can be indoors or outdoors; you might find a bargain there
8 something that has existed for an extensive period of time

2 Complete the text with the correct options, A, B or C.

What does tradition mean to you?

It's important for me to ¹ ___ cultural and family traditions. I've got my own favourites. We moved to our house on January 1st five years ago, so it's really easy to remember that date and every New Year's Day, we ² ___ the occasion with a special barbecue and invite our friends and neighbours to join us. There's another special date in March when we make statues of famous people and parade them around the streets! Nobody knows the ³ ___ of this tradition, but it's fun. If that falls ⁴ ___ a weekend we move the holiday to the nearest weekday. There are local dishes we eat at this time. Our town used to be a simple fishing village, and the food is a ⁵ ___ of our history.

1 A uphold   B hold up   C holding
2 A mark   B make   C move
3 A originals B openings   C origins
4 A on   B at   C in
5 A recall   B reminder   C remember

3 Choose a word or phrase from the vocabulary on this page to match the answers to the question *What does tradition mean to you?*

1 Because I work at the festival, tradition means a long time collecting the rubbish and putting things in order the day after!
2 It means a special day when our daughters or sons becomes adults.
3 Our local council spends a lot or money on things we don't need.
4 Something that I will do in a totally different way this year.

→ YOUR TURN

4 Think about your experiences of celebrations and/or your feelings about traditions. Find two more new words to describe some of them. Write them here.

UNIT 7 MY VOCABULARY

Can you remember the vocabulary from Unit 7?
Use the letters and the number of letters to help you.

ADJECTIVES WITH DEPENDANT PREPOSITIONS

1 a _ _ _ _ _ _ _ _ _   t _ (10,2)
2 c _ _ _ _ _ _ _ _ _   t _ (10,2)
3 d _ _ _ _ _ _ _ _   t _ (9,2)
4 d _ _ _ _ _ _ _ _ _ _ _ _   b _ (13,2)
5 h _ _ _ _ _   t _ (7,2)
6 i _ _ _ _ _ _ _ _ _ _ _ _   f _ _ (13,3)
7 i _ _ _ _ _ _   t _ (8,2)
8 i _ _ _ _ _ _   b _ (8,2)
9 k _ _ _ _ _ _ _ _ _ _ _ _   a _ _ _ _ (13,5)
10 s _ _ _ _ _ _ _   t _ (8,2)
11 s _ _ _ _ _ _ _ _   o _ (10,2)
12 u _ _ _ _ _ _ _ _ _ _   t _ (11,2)

IDIOMS

13 p _ _ _   i _   t _ _   n _ _ _ _ (4,2,3,4)
14 e _ _ _ _ _   s _ _ _   t _ _ _   d _ _ _ (6,4,4,4)
15 f _ _ _ _   t _ _   m _ _ _ _ (4,3,5)
16 g _   h _ _ _   i _   h _ _ _ (2,4,2,4)
17 i _ _   n _ _ _ _ _ _ _ _ (2,1,8)
18 s _ _   t _ _   r _ _ _ _ _   s _ _ _ _ _ _ _ _ (3,3,6,8)
19 t _ _ _ _   something   a _   f _ _ _ _   v _ _ _ _ (4,2,4,5)
20 t _ _   b _ _ _   o _   b _ _ _   w _ _ _ _ _ _ (3,4,2,4,6)
21 t _ _ _ _   b _ _ _ _ _   e _ _ (4,1,5,3)

VOCABULARY EXTENSION

1 Read the text and complete the definitions 1–8 with the underlined words and phrases in the text.

> When I started doing research, I was praised for my efforts. Self-confidence has never been my <u>strong point</u>, so that meant a lot to me. The project that produced the breakthrough happened almost by accident. In our team, no idea was ever <u>dismissed</u>, nothing was <u>worthless</u> until there was proof it didn't work, <u>regardless of</u> how crazy an idea seemed. I was so lucky to be part of a group with <u>vision</u>. Of course, without fundings we couldn't do our work, but the university <u>kept our work going</u> even when we weren't getting results. Once we had our first success, we were able to <u>determine</u> how to develop what would <u>lie ahead</u> in the project.

1 _____ is a way of saying *in spite of*.
2 _____ means to decide what will happen.
3 _____ (verb) means decide that something or someone is not important or worth considering.
4 A _____ is a particular skill or ability that a person or an organisation has.
5 _____ is the ability to make imaginative plans for the future.
6 If you _____, you keep making something happen or operate.
7 Something _____ (adjective) is not important or useful.
8 _____ means an event or situation that will happen in the future, with either a negative or positive outcome.

2 Complete the text about science fiction with a word or expression from the box.

> best of both worlds   comparable to
> hand in hand   hostile to   in a nutshell
> knowledgeable about   lies ahead
> strong point   turn a blind eye

People who are ¹_____ science fiction suggest we can identify 'clean future' and 'dirty future' themes in the genre. 'Clean future' themes are very positive about what ²_____: technology will make our lives better and progress and space exploration will go ³_____ with peace and understanding. We will have the ⁴_____.
'Dirty future' themes, on the other hand, are ⁵_____ the idea of science controlling our lives. They imagine a world where powerful corporations own everything and governments ⁶_____ to what they do. 'Clean' and 'dirty', it has been suggested, are really a reflection of the present, ⁷_____ a mirror in which we look critically at ourselves. ⁸_____, the more optimistic we are, the better the future looks. This means a ⁹_____ of sci-fi as a genre is that it asks questions about how we live now and the impact that could have on the future.

→ YOUR TURN

3 Find two more new words related to the future. They might be about your own ideas, or aspects of technology and science. Write them here, with a translation or a description of the meaning.

UNIT 8 MY VOCABULARY

Can you remember the vocabulary from Unit 8? Use the letters and the number of letters to help you.

ADJECTIVES WITH PREFIXES

1. a _ _ _ _ _ _ _ _ _ _ (11)
2. d _ _ _ _ _ _ _ _ _ _ _ _ _ (14)
3. m _ _ _ _ _ _ (7)
4. n _ _ _ _ _ _ _ _ _ (10)
5. h _ _ _ _ _ _ _ _ _ _ _ _ (13)
6. o _ _ _ _ _ _ _ (8)
7. p _ _ _ _ _ _ (7)
8. p _ _ _ - i _ _ _ _ _ _ _ _ _ (3,10)
9. r _ _ _ _ _ _ _ _ (9)
10. s _ _ _ _ - p _ _ _ _ _ _ _ _ (4,9)
11. u _ _ _ _ - e _ _ _ _ _ _ _ _ (5,9)
12. u _ _ _ _ _ _ _ _ _ _ (11)
13. s _ _ _ _ - w _ _ _ (4,4)
14. a _ _ _ _ _ _ _ _ _ _ _ _ _ _ (15)
15. p _ _ _ _ _ _ _ _ _ _ (11)
16. p _ _ _ _ _ _ _ _ _ _ _ (12)
17. d _ _ _ _ _ _ _ (8)
18. u _ _ _ _ _ _ _ _ _ _ _ _ _ (14)
19. u _ _ _ _ - c _ _ _ _ _ _ _ (5,7)
20. h _ _ _ _ _ _ _ _ _ _ (11)
21. m _ _ _ _ _ _ (7)
22. o _ _ _ _ _ _ _ _ _ (10)
23. r _ _ _ _ _ _ _ _ _ _ (11)
24. n _ _ _ _ _ _ _ _ (9)

THE ANIMAL KINGDOM

25. c _ _ _ /w _ _ _ - b _ _ _ _ _ _ _ _ (4,4,8)
26. f _ _ _ _ _ (6)
27. m _ _ _ _ _ (6)
28. s _ _ _ _ _ (6)
29. i _ c _ _ _ _ _ _ _ _ (2,9)
30. m _ _ _ _ _ (6)
31. m _ _ _ _ _ _ _ _ (9)
32. n _ _ _ _ _ _ _ h _ _ _ _ _ _ (7,7)
33. p _ _ _ _ _ _ _ (8)
34. p _ _ _ (4)

VOCABULARY EXTENSION

1 Read the web article about a sustainability movement. Replace the underlined words and phrases in the text with the words in the box.

> emerged   evolve   fulfil these functions
> movement   mutual   no harm in
> takes on board   the will

Home | **Articles**

New ideas and theories about how humans and the natural world interact are appearing all the time. Today, I want to focus on a movement called Solarpunk. Solarpunk is different in some way because it has [1] <u>appeared</u> as a positive and hopeful [2] <u>group of people with a particular set of aims or ideas</u> that believes humans, the natural world and responsible technology can have [3] <u>common</u> benefits. It [4] <u>understands and accepts</u> the practical issues of how to provide food and resources but also thinks science can [5] <u>perform the tasks</u> without damaging the environment. This might all seem very idealistic, but there's [6] <u>no argument against</u> looking at what Solarpunk is suggesting – that human beings can achieve great things through [7] <u>what we want to happen</u> and determination to [8] <u>develop</u> new and better ways of coexisting with the natural world.

2 Complete the memoir extract with 'Animal Kingdom' vocabulary and vocabulary from Exercise 1.

People who have only ever seen animals [1] _____ are often totally unprepared for the experience of seeing them in their [2] _____. There's a world of difference. It's really important to [3] _____ the fact that you are on their territory, not the other way round. It can also be quite a shock to see animals attack, hunt and eat one another. But these complex relationships and roles of [4] _____ and [5] _____ are part of a natural relationship that has [6] _____ over incredibly long periods of time. However, this is only part of the story. When I started work at the nature reserve, I was constantly amazed at the beauty of the world around me. Watching a [7] _____ tiger playing gently with its cubs or the annual [8] _____ of thousands of birds as they began their long journeys to another continent are truly unforgettable moments.

➡ YOUR TURN

3 Find two more new words related to the future. They might be about your own ideas, aspects of the animal kingdom or adjectives with prefixes. Write them here, with a translation or a description of the meaning.

UNIT 9 MY VOCABULARY

Can you remember the vocabulary from Unit 9? Use the letters and the number of letters to help you.

TRAVEL – COLLOCATIONS AND PHRASES

1 b _ _ _ _   t _ _   j _ _ _ _ _ _ _ (5,3,7)
2 d _ t _ _   s _ _ _ _ _ (2,3,6)
3 c _ _ _   t _ _ _   s _ _ _ _ _ _ _ _ _ _ (4,2,1,10)
4 g _ _   a _ _ _   f _ _ _ _   i _   a _ _ (3,4,5,2,3)
5 a _ _ -i _ _ _ _ _ _ _ _ _   r _ _ _ _ _ (3,9,6)
6 c _ _ _ _ _ _ _   f _ _ _ _ _ (7,6)
7 f _ _ _   b _ _ _ _ (4,5)
8 h _ _ _   b _ _ _ _ (4,5)
9 h _ _ _ _ _ _ _   o _   _   l _ _ _ _ _ _ _ (7,2,1,8)
10 p _ _ _ _ _ _   h _ _ _ _ _ _ (7,7)
11 s _ _ _ -c _ _ _ _ _ _ _ _   a _ _ _ _ _ _ _ _ _ _ _ _ _ (4,8,13)
12 s _ _ _ _ _ _ _ _   f _ _ _ _ _ (9,6)

TRAVEL IDIOMS

13 b _ _ _   o _   t _ _ _ _ (4,2,5)
14 b _   p _ _ _ _ _   s _ _ _ _ _ _ _ (2,5,7)
15 c _ _ _ _ _   t _ _ _   b _ _ _ _ _ _ (when I/you/...)   c _ _ _ _   t _ _   i _ _) (5,4,6,4,2,2)
16 d _ _   U- _ _ _ _ _ (2,1,5)
17 d _ _ _   t _ _ _   l _ _ _ _ (4,3,4)
18 f _ _ _ _ _ _   h _ _ _ _ (6,4)
19 g _ _ /h _ _ _   i _ _ _ _ _   f _ _ _ (3/4,5,4)
20 r _ _ _   o _ _   o _ _   s _ _ _ _ _ (3,3,2,5)

VOCABULARY EXTENSION

1 **Read the online article and match the underlined words and phrases to the definitions 1–10.**

> **Our weekly series *One Sentence Please* asked 'What does – or should – it mean to be a tourist nowadays?' Here is a selection of your answers.**
>
> It should be an opportunity to learn about other countries and cultures through an <u>authentic</u> experience and that might mean going to a <u>rough</u> city or somewhere that doesn't have comfortable hotels and fast-food restaurants.
>
> It seems to be <u>squeezing through crowds</u> and spending a fortune on a cup of coffee just to take a photo to post on social media.
>
> It's a way of being <u>selective</u> about the place you visit, I only want to see the historic buildings, the beautiful landscapes and <u>stroll through</u> the lovely old neighbourhoods but avoid the <u>overcrowded</u>, typical attractions.
>
> It's another form of <u>consumption</u> – just another thing to spend money on because you can.
>
> It should <u>broaden</u> your awareness of how others live by meeting real, <u>down-to-earth</u> people who represent their communities.
>
> Tourists are <u>looked on as</u> a source of income, like they're walking cash machines!

1 considered
2 practical, reasonable and friendly
3 extend
4 dangerous
5 walk in a slow, relaxed way
6 the amount used
7 move with difficulty due to the number of people
8 real, true
9 containing too many people or things
10 intentionally choosing some things and not others

2 **Complete the travel website advertisement with the correct options.**

> Deals   Destinations   Search …
>
> Are you looking for the holiday ¹*of / from / in* a lifetime, or just a few days to get away ²*of / from / with* it all in some quiet, relaxing spot? Do you look on travel as an adventure, full of surprises, or do you want a stress-free beak where everything is ³*still / soft / plain* sailing staying at a(n) ⁴*all / total / full*-inclusive resort? Is your aim to visit the big city and ⁵*make / get / do* all the sights, or are you more interested is strolling ⁶*up / through / over* the peaceful streets of a small, country village? At TrueTours we provide the perfect holiday according to your needs and preferences. Find out more and find the perfect holiday on our website now.

→ YOUR TURN

3 **Find two more new words related to travel. Write them here, with a translation or a description of the meaning.**

TOWARDS PROFICIENCY

TOWARDS PROFICIENCY 1

BOOK IDIOMS

1 Look at the extract from an online magazine. What do the quiz questions tell you about someone's personality?

> It's national book week, so this week's personality quiz has a 'books and reading' theme.
>
> Are you <u>an open book</u> or <u>a closed book</u>?
> Find out with today's quiz.
>
> 1 Do your friends say they can <u>read you like a book</u>?
> 2 When you meet someone and don't like them, do you tell yourself <u>you can't judge a book by its cover</u>?
> 3 If you have a problem, do you <u>take it as read</u> that your friends will help you?
> 4 Are you the kind of person who reads instructions <u>from cover to cover</u>?
> 5 When talking to close friends about their problems, are you good at <u>reading between the lines</u>?
> 6 When you follow a process, do you feel happier <u>doing things by the book</u>, or improvising as you go along?

2 Match the answers a–f to questions 1–6 in Exercise 1.

a Absolutely. Every single word and page. And sometimes twice!
b I am very empathetic, so I can often tell how someone is feeling even if they don't tell me directly.
c Oh yes. They know I can't be something I'm not.
d I do, although maybe I shouldn't. I mean you can take people for granted, can't you?
e I like having the freedom to experiment, but I know that's not always a good idea.
f I try to, because some people are shy and take a while to warm up.

3 Match the underlined idioms from the quiz to the definitions.

1 a person or thing that is difficult to understand
2 don't assume you know what someone/ something is like based on their appearance
3 accept or assume that something is true without checking
4 someone whose thoughts and feelings are easy to understand
5 understand someone's motives easily
6 try to understand someone's real feelings or intentions from what they say or write
7 do things exactly as the rules say they should be done
8 read something from beginning to end

4 Complete the dialogues with a word from the box. There is one word you do not need to use.

> between   by   closed
> from   judge   open   take

1 A: He didn't say it, but I knew what he meant.
   B: You've always been good at reading _____ the lines.
2 A: You read the whole thing? Even the index?
   B: Well yes, I like to read books _____ cover to cover.
3 A: He can't hide his feelings.
   B: I know sometimes it's a bit embarrassing – he's such an _____ book.
4 A: The film had glowing reviews, but that doesn't necessarily mean it's good.
   B: Oh, I don't know, she's such a good director you can _____ it as read the film will be good.
5 A: My science teacher insists that we follow the procedure exactly.
   B: I see why, you've got to do things _____ the book.
6 A: I don't like the look of that pizzeria – it's very dark in there!
   B: Oh don't _____ a book by its cover – the food's great, I promise you.

OVER TO YOU

5 Choose three of the questions from the personality quiz. Write answers to them using the idioms in Exercise 1.

TOWARDS PROFICIENCY 2

TALKING ABOUT THE FUTURE: IDIOMS AND EXPRESSIONS

1 Angie Furlong is the new coach of the Hyde Eagles FC. Read part of her recent press conference. How confident does she seem about the team's chances for the new season?

Journalist 1: Hyde were on the brink of going down to League Two last season. Will you make a lot of changes?

Angie: Right now, I'm focused on getting to know the players. We <u>make a start</u> next week with a friendly game against the Lions, so that's my priority.

Journalist 2: Hi Angie. The fans are excited about your arrival. You've been called <u>the light at the end of the tunnel</u>. How do you feel about that?

Angie: Hyde has great fans and it's an honour to be here. But I ask everyone to be patient. Success takes time. I can't tell you it's just <u>around the corner</u>, but what I can tell you is that we expect 100% from the whole team and my aim is to restore confidence.

Journalist 1: Does that mean you're <u>setting your sights</u> on survival rather than winning the league?

Angie: I always want to win. Every game. It's about attitude.

Journalist 3: I think everyone knows you were about to be offered the job of coaching the national under-21 women's team. Were you disappointed not to get it?

Angie: You can't have regrets in this business. If you do, you <u>run the risk</u> of being distracted. My job is to <u>think ahead</u> and take Hyde back to the top division.

Journalist 2: We are waiting <u>with bated breath</u> to see which new players you will add to the team. It's known you have been looking at several goalkeepers, will you <u>take the plunge</u> and buy Maria Serra from Milan?

Angie: I can't comment on that at present. Any other questions?

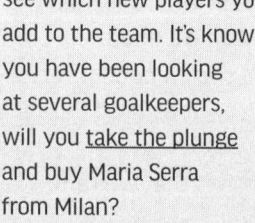
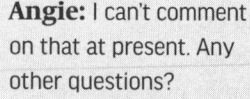

2 Match the underlined expressions in the interview to the defintions 1–8.

1 do something although something bad might happen because of it
2 something that is going to happen very soon
3 make plans for things you want to do
4 make a decision to do something you're nervous about, especially after thinking about it a lot
5 in a nervous or excited way
6 begin
7 signs of improvement in a situation that has been bad for a long time
8 decide to achieve something

3 Match the sentence halves.

1 The club needs a new stadium, the owners should
2 Buying and spending a lot on new players is
3 It's really good to have someone who
4 I'm excited that the tournament cup
5 I'm going to support the team this year although

a thinks ahead and has long-term plans.
b a month ago I was on the brink of giving up on them.
c is just around the corner.
d running the risk of getting into debt.
e take the plunge and build one.

4 Complete the sentences with the correct phrase (a–e).

1 I'm so excited about seeing the first match and I'm ___ to see who she picks for the team.
2 Winning our first two games of the season might be ___ after last year's failures.
3 If I were the coach, I think I'd ___ and pick some of the young players from the junior team.
4 I'm sure the team has ___ finishing the season on the top five in the league.
5 If you don't buy the tickets now you ___ of not getting a seat for the game.

a take the plunge
b the light at the end of the tunnel
c run the risk
d waiting with bated breath
e set their sights on

OVER TO YOU

5 Think about times when you made – or thought about making – decisions about the future. Perhaps you changed your mind, had a good plan or objective – maybe you thought about the dangers or felt optimistic.

Choose three of the expressions from this page and write sentences about your experiences.

TOWARDS PROFICIENCY 3
TRAVEL IDIOMS

1 Read the messages from friends on very different holidays. Who is most positive about their experience so far?

Hi, Jan. How's it going? We got here this morning. That's right! This morning. It was an <u>arduous journey</u>. We got up at <u>the crack of dawn</u> and set off for the airport. The weather was terrible, and really windy. So windy in fact that they <u>diverted</u> our flight to Santiago. The problem was, there was no connecting flight until the next morning and we had to sleep in the airport. The airline gave us vouchers for some basic food – but it was hardly enough for a small sandwich. As you know, we're travelling <u>on a shoestring</u> so we couldn't afford much – airport prices are so expensive! And then we had to walk from one end of the building to the other. Luckily, we're <u>travelling light</u> so at least we didn't have heavy cases. But now we're here, the weather is glorious and views are breathtaking. The adventure begins!

Hey Issa. Wow! I've never had your <u>thirst for adventure</u> but that sounds brilliant – despite the problems with the journey. We came here by train – you know my dad won't fly now because of the environment, and everything went smoothly (unlike your trip). I thought I would miss the <u>hustle and bustle</u> of Madrid here, but I don't really – well, not a lot! This kind of nature holiday isn't my thing, as you know, but I decided to just <u>go with the flow</u>, and I'm enjoying the experience. There's a lot of walking though! The lakes are only a couple of kilometres from our hotel (more like a hut!) <u>as the crow flies</u> but it takes almost two hours to walk there through the forest. Annie's totally into bird watching so she <u>keeps her eyes peeled</u> for rare species and we have to stop all the time. Who knows, maybe I'll come back a bird fan? That would surprise you!

2 Match the underlined expressions in the text to the definitions 1–10.
1 really want new experiences
2 the day begins
3 the easiest route
4 directed to an unplanned location
5 do what other people are doing
6 without much money
7 not take much with you
8 a difficult trip
9 watch carefully for someone or something
10 a lot of noise and activity

3 Complete the text with the correct form of an expression from Exercise 2.

It was no surprise to my parents when I told them my plan to travel to Asia and Australasia. They know I have a ¹_____ – ever since I was child I've wanted to see other countries. I made plans and saved up enough money for a flight, but planned to travel ²_____ as I only had a small amount left for the rest of the trip. Coming from a very quiet village I was shocked at the ³_____ of crowded Asian cities, but I quickly learnt the importance of ⁴_____. I just tried to do the same as everyone else. Because I was ⁵_____ with just a small backpack, it was easy to get around. The highlight of my travels was the Australian outback. I went with a small group of people I got friendly with when our flight ⁶_____ and we spent half a day at the airport. Getting to the outback was an ⁷_____ that took several days, not so far ⁸_____, but we didn't take a direct route. We set off at the ⁹_____ to make the most of the day. I always ¹⁰_____ for animals because I wanted to see as much wildlife as possible.

OVER TO YOU

4 Choose three of the expressions from this page and write sentences about your ideas, experiences or travel plans for the future.

TOWARDS PROFICIENCY 4

DESCRIBING PERSONALITY: IDIOMS AND ADJECTIVES

1 **Read the email reviewing two candidates for the position of team leader for a school open-day. Who would you choose, Elli or Simon?**

Inbox — 2 Messages

From: M. Sumner   **To:** the open-day committee

In order to decide whether Elli or Simon should be chosen as the team-leader for the annual school open-day, I have summarised the feedback from people who have worked with them in the past, asking what characteristics the candidates displayed. I hope the following comments help you when making your decision.

Elli has an enthusiastic and <u>bubbly</u> personality which makes her popular. She's very capable and has a lot of surprising skills, in fact she's a bit of <u>a dark horse</u> who is good at problem-solving. However, she can be rather <u>impulsive</u> and doesn't always listen to adivce. Some people who work with her also say she <u>has a stubborn streak</u>. While that's not always a bad thing as it's important to be determined, she can also be <u>ruthless</u> – she'll do anything to get what she wants. To conclude, she has <u>displayed leadership qualities</u> in the past and could be a very good choice.

Simon is really <u>meticulous</u>. He's great with details and would help his team make plans and set deadlines. However, I've heard he has an <u>abrasive personality</u> when he's really focused, and some people have complained he can be <u>downright rude</u>. Personally, I've always found him caring and <u>courteous</u>, so that surprised me. He's got a very <u>sharp wit</u>, so perhaps he upsets people sometimes when he thinks he's being funny but they think he's criticising them. He has less leadership experience than Elli but is the kind of person who responds well to a challenge, and he's <u>a mine of information</u> on all kinds of subjects.

2 **Match the underlined expressions in the email to the definitions 1–12.**

1 show a typical quality that makes someone different from another (Elli)
2 polite (Simon)
3 not thinking or worrying about any pain caused to others (Elli)
4 very careful and with great attention to detail (Simon)
5 someone who keeps their interests and ideas secret, especially a surprising ability or skill (Elli)
6 happy and enthusiastic character (Elli)
7 very impolite (Simon)
8 doing things suddenly without any planning and without considering the effects they may have (Elli)
9 behave in a rude harsh or unpleasant way (Simon)
10 someone who knows a lot about a subject or subjects (Simon)
11 the ability to say clever, amusing things (Simon)
12 a quality of someone's character (often negative) when they are determined not to change their mind (Elli)

3 **Read what some classmates said about Simon and Elli and decide who they are talking about. Choose words and phrases from Exercise 2 to support your choice.**

She/He …
1 checks their work over and over again.
2 is incapable of accepting that some things just can't be done.
3 is always smiling and telling us about funny things that happened.
4 sometimes doesn't even say 'hello' when I walk into the room.
5 fixed my PC. Brilliant with tech. Who would have guessed?
6 knows all about the history of the school right back to the last century.

OVER TO YOU

4 **Choose three of the expressions from this page and write sentences to describe yourself or someone you know.**

TOWARDS PROFICIENCY 5

REPORTING WHAT PEOPLE SAY

1 Match the reporting verbs in the box to the definitions.

> acquiesce applaud concede contend
> dispute hint recollect ridicule uphold vow

1 remember
2 defend a decision or right
3 agree to something, often when you don't want to
4 accept
5 promise
6 say that something is true
7 suggest something in an indirect way
8 disagree
9 to approve of or admire
10 laugh at someone in an unkind way

2 Mark and Petra work in the same project team. Mark has accused Petra of taking his ideas and presenting them as her own. Read what they said to their supervisor, then complete the supervisor's report with verbs from Exercise 1.

Mark: I want to complain about Petra stealing my ideas. I'm pretty sure she's been reading my notebooks – I remember her asking to check things from my notes a couple of times, but I didn't think anything of it. We're working on the same project, after all. But now I want to see all her notes. Sure, I know I can be a bit possessive about my ideas, but I'm sure she copied them and don't accept her explanation.

Petra: I can promise you that I've never taken Mark's notebooks. There's no way I'm going to accept this accusation and give him all my work to look at – why should I? I suggest you interview the rest of the team and see what their experiences with him are; you might be surprised. In addition, we all have the right to refer to each other's research, that's allowed. He sometimes laughs at my ideas, but I'm perfectly capable of making as many breakthroughs as a brilliant innovator like him.

Mark ¹_____ that Petra has been reading his notebooks. He ²_____ her asking to borrow his notes. Furthermore, he ³_____ her claim that what happened was just a coincidence. He ⁴_____ that he can be rather possessive about his ideas, but insists she stole them.
Petra ⁵_____ she has never taken Mark's books and won't ⁶_____ to his demand to see her notes. She ⁷_____ that other members of the team might have comments relevant to this situation. Petra also ⁸_____ the right of team members to look at each other's work. She complains that Mark sometimes ⁹_____ her ideas. On the other hand, she ¹⁰_____ his ability as an innovator.

3 Use the verb in brackets to report these comments.

0 I am sure it was Jamie who told me the meeting was going to be on Monday. (RECOLLECT)
He recollects Jamie telling him the meeting is on Monday.

1 If you tell me which day you want to go to the concert, I might know someone who can get you tickets. (HINT)
2 You were right. I thought Mozart was German, but Wikipedia says he was Austrian. (CONCEDE)
3 I can give you my word that I never revealed your secret to anyone. (VOW)
4 The judge confirmed that we have the right to use the lake for swimming because it is not private property. (UPHOLD)
5 I congratulate you on your generous decision to donate the money you made at the school fair to a local charity. (APPLAUD)

OVER TO YOU

4 Imagine a situation where you have to report a conversation between two team members. Write three sentences about it using verbs from Exercise 1.

TOWARDS PROFICIENCY 6

THERE IS AND *IT IS* EXPRESSIONS

1 Read the online college forum. What do the questions have in common?

Home >   Advice ⌄

1 Q: I've seen that the college has a scheme for lending students' computers during their course. That would certainly interest me as I don't have a PC, and they are pretty expensive. Do you recommend applying for one?

A: Absolutely. They are very good models and there's <u>no point in</u> spending money on a computer if you don't have to. <u>It's no wonder</u> lots of students are taking advantage of this scheme.

---

2 Q: I've recently been receiving a lot of publicity from local banks. Why is that and should I open an account with one of them?

A: <u>It's no surprise</u> that you're getting contacted by local banks as they always try to attract new students and persuade them to open an account. But <u>there's no need to</u> do anything until you have considered all the options. And you can always ask the student financial advisor to help you choose.

---

3 Q: I've seen the college offers some grants to help students with their research costs. As a new student, do I qualify?

A: Probably not, these grants are mostly for final year students, but there's <u>no harm in</u> trying!

---

4 Q: How can I call the student financial advisor? There's no number. <u>It's no use</u> having this service if I can't get in touch with them! It's so frustrating.

A: <u>There's no denying</u> the way of arranging to talk to the advisor is a bit complicated, but <u>there's no reason to</u> feel frustrated. If you make an appointment through the free app they'll see you straight away.

---

5 Q: The cost of accommodation is very expensive and I'm finding it difficult to make ends meet. I've seen some department stores have vacancies for sales staff at the weekend. Should I apply? I could certainly do with the extra money.

A: <u>There's no doubt</u> that the cost of living has increased in the last few years, and I understand your situation. However, you must make sure you can meet deadlines with a weekend job. If you see <u>there is no alternative but to</u> work at the weekend, discuss the situation with your tutor.

---

2 Match the questions 1–5 in Exercise 1 to a–f below. Sometimes more than one answer is possible.

According to the advice, who …
- a should bear time considerations in mind?
- b shouldn't do something in a rush?
- c can be confident of quality?
- d can resolve their problem swiftly?
- e is unlikely to be successful?
- f can easily obtain expert advice?

3 Complete the rules. Use the underlined expressions in Exercise 1 to help you.

1 *There's no need / There is no reason* followed by _____ + infinitive.
2 *It's no use/ There's no point (in) / There's no harm (in)* followed by the _____ form.
3 *There's no alternative* is followed by *but + to* + _____ .

4 Use the word in brackets and the underlined expressions from Exercise 1 to rephrase the sentences 1–10.

1 It's a waste of time asking him to contribute to the charity – he's really mean. (POINT)
2 My friend Angie was very lucky to get such a well-paid job at such a young age. (DENYING)
3 You can ask them if they give student discounts on books; they might say yes. (HARM)
4 Buying the more expensive camera was definitely a good decision considering how many extra features it has. (DOUBT)
5 As you can't buy that locally, you will have to order it online. (ALTERNATIVE)
6 The trainers were such a bargain. I totally understand why you bought them. (WONDER)
7 They don't expect you to pay a deposit on the bike. (NEED)
8 I can't pay with my card as there's no money in my account. (USE)
9 I always knew she would choose to study economics at university. (SURPRISE)
10 Don't worry about the prices – we will share the cost of the meal. (REASON)

OVER TO YOU

5 Choose three of the expressions from this page and write your own sentences.

IRREGULAR VERBS

Infinitive	Past simple	Past participle	Translation	Infinitive	Past simple	Past participle	Translation
be	was/were	been		leave	left	left	
beat	beat	beaten		lend	lent	lent	
become	became	become		let	let	let	
begin	began	begun		lie	lied	lied	
bite	bit	bitten		light	lit	lit	
bleed	bled	bled		lose	lost	lost	
blow	blew	blown		make	made	made	
break	broke	broken		mean	meant	meant	
bring	brought	brought		meet	met	met	
build	built	built		pay	paid	paid	
burn	burned/burnt	burned/burnt		put	put	put	
buy	bought	bought		read	read	read	
catch	caught	caught		ride	rode	ridden	
choose	chose	chosen		ring	rang	rung	
come	came	come		rise	rose	risen	
cost	cost	cost		run	ran	run	
cut	cut	cut		say	said	said	
dig	dug	dug		see	saw	seen	
do	did	done		sell	sold	sold	
draw	drew	drawn		send	sent	sent	
dream	dreamed/dreamt	dreamed/dreamt		shine	shone	shone	
drink	drank	drunk		shoot	shot	shot	
drive	drove	driven		show	showed	shown	
eat	ate	eaten		shut	shut	shut	
fall	fell	fallen		sing	sang	sung	
feel	felt	felt		sit	sat	sat	
fight	fought	fought		sleep	slept	slept	
find	found	found		speak	spoke	spoken	
fly	flew	flown		spell	spelled/spelt	spelled/spelt	
forget	forgot	forgotten		spend	spent	spent	
get	got	got		stand	stood	stood	
give	gave	given		steal	stole	stolen	
go	went	gone		swim	swam	swum	
grow	grew	grown		take	took	taken	
hang	hung	hung		teach	taught	taught	
have	had	had		tear	tore	torn	
hear	heard	heard		tell	told	told	
hide	hid	hidden		think	thought	thought	
hit	hit	hit		throw	threw	thrown	
hold	held	held		understand	understood	understood	
hurt	hurt	hurt		wake	woke	woken	
keep	kept	kept		wear	wore	worn	
know	knew	known		win	won	won	
lead	led	led		write	wrote	written	
learn	learned/learnt	learned/learnt					

Acknowledgements

The authors and publishers acknowledge the following sources of copyright material and are grateful for the permissions granted. While every effort has been made, it has not always been possible to identify the sources of all the material used, or to trace all copyright holders. If any omissions are brought to our notice, we will be happy to include the appropriate acknowledgements on reprinting and in the next update to the digital edition, as applicable.

The publishers are grateful to the following contributors: EMC Design Ltd, text design and layouts; Daniel Summersgill, cover design; Sonica Studios, audio recordings; Daniel Brint, Exploring Employability, Vocabulary Builder and Towards Proficiency sections author; Nicola Foufouti, Rebecca Raynes, Ruth Cox, Editorial work; Jill Buggey, Joanna Kosta, exam review.

Key: U = Unit, Review = R.

Texts

U5: The Guardian for the text adapted from 'The big idea: your personality is not set in stone' by David Robson, *The Guardian*, 13.02.2023. Copyright © 2023 Guardian News & Media Limited. Reproduced with permission; **U7:** The Guardian for the text adapted from 'The flow state: the science of the elusive creative mindset that can improve your life' by David Robson, *The Guardian,* 20.07.2024. Copyright © 2024 Guardian News & Media Limited. Reproduced with permission; The Guardian for the text adapted from 'It's nice to help a life to live: meet Sri Lanka's turtle guardians' by Dimuthu Attanayake, *The Guardian,* 08.08.2024. Copyright © 2024 Guardian News & Media Limited. Reproduced with permission; The Guardian for the text adapted from "It shouldn't be a bucket list place': these people went to Antarctica. They hope you don't' by Sarah Aitken. *The Guardian*, 08.08.2024. Copyright © 2024 Guardian News & Media Limited. Reproduced with permission.

Photography

All the photographs are sourced from Getty Images.

U1: piranka/E+; Abdul Rauf/iStock; d3sign/Moment; VioletaStoimenova/E+; oxygen/Moment; Jenny Meilihove/Moment; Qweek/E+; **U2:** Alistair Berg/DigitalVision; Luis Alvarez/DigitalVision; Sorin Banica/500px; peepo/E+; artyme83/iStock/Getty Images Plus; Goodboy Picture Company/E+; **U3:** Francesco Carta fotografo/Moment; rubberball/Rubberball Productions; Alpov/iStock/Getty Images Plus; imv/E+; Bob Lord/iStock Editorial; MoMo Productions/DigitalVision; Bajak/E+; EkaterinaKu/iStock/Getty Images Plus; **U4:** Commercial Eye/The Image Bank; Sean Anthony Eddy/E+; Carol Yepes/Moment; Deepak Sethi/E+; leventince/E+; Sean Gladwell/Moment; ViewApart/iStock/Getty Images Plus; Nikada/E+; Elena Medoks/Moment; GaryAlvis/E+; Aldis Ozols/500Px Plus; hadynyah/E+; 'Christian Kober/robertharding/Collection Mix: Subjects; **U5:** Image Source/Photodisc; Taiyou Nomachi/Stone; Nikola Stojadinovic/E+; Ron Levine/DigitalVision; martin-dm/E+; **U6:** tekinturkdogan/iStock/Getty Images Plus; Luis Alvarez/DigitalVision; Patrick Chu/E+; urbazon/E+; Westend61; Tony Anderson/DigitalVision; SolStock/E+; British Modern Photography/Moment; Caiaimage/Robert Daly/iStock/Getty Images Plus; Reza Estakhrian/The Image Bank; **U7:** Edward Langley/Moment; EyeEm Mobile GmbH/iStock/Getty Images Plus; zf L/Moment; iantfoto/E+; Nazar Rybak/iStock/Getty Images Plus; Sergey Mironov/Moment; gorodenkoff/iStock; monkeybusinessimages/iStock/Getty Images Plus; **U8:** SolStock/E+; Westend61; Stephen Frink/The Image Bank; Antonio Hugo Photo/Moment; shellgrit/iStock/Getty Images Plus; Alessandro De Maddalena/iStock/Getty Images Plus; kellyvandellen/iStock/Getty Images Plus; David McGowen/iStock/Getty Images Plus; bluejayphoto/iStock/Getty Images Plus; Andrey Danilovich/E+; oversnap/E+; ollo/iStock Unreleased; Geography Photos/Universal Images Group; Tassii/E+; Drazen_/E+; **R1:** Perawit Boonchu/iStock; georgeclerk/E+; **R2:** mikkelwilliam/E+; Goodboy Picture Company/E+; Andriy Onufriyenko/Moment; **R3:** mister Big/iStock/Getty Images Plus; **Exploring Employability:** skynesher/E+; Drazen Zigic/iStock/Getty Images Plus; mixetto/E+; Cavan Images/Drentwett Niedring; martinedoucet/E+; Thomas Barwick/DigitalVision; Funkey Factory/iStock/Getty Images Plus; Morsa Images/DigitalVision; Morsa Images/DigitalVision; Tom Werner/DigitalVision; Maria Stavreva/DigitalVision Vectors; skynesher/E+; andresr/E+; Hemera Technologies/AbleStock.com; HappyKids/E+; Cavan Images; Tetra Images/Tetra images; Enis Aksoy/DigitalVision Vectors; courtneyk/E+; Tempura/E+; coastalrunner/iStock Editorial; Jordan Siemens/DigitalVision; blackCAT/E+; Maskot/DigitalVision; Tegra Stone Nuess; kali9/E+; FluxFactory/E+.

Cover photography by RyanJLane/E+/Getty Images.

Audio

Audios produced by Sonica Studios Ltd.

Typeset

Typesetting by EMC Design Ltd.

URLs

The publisher has used its best endeavours to ensure that the URLs for external websites referred to in this book are correct and active at the time of going to press. However, the publisher has no responsibility for the websites and can make no guarantee that a site will remain live or that the content is or will remain appropriate.